MW01122839

"Mandy Urena's memoir, *TOUCHY, FEELY, SQUEEZY: MUSINGS OF A MASSEUSE*, is a delightful, insightful, and candid account of one woman's journey of self-discovery through the magic of massage. Urena takes us with her on a rich assortment of wild and poignant escapades all over the world. Her musings are sprinkled with wit and have the added surprise of genuine sentimentality, fodder for deep reflection. I was sad when I finished the book, for I wanted to continue with her on more adventures. Thanks to Urena for her honest and thoughtful tales, sure to inspire readers to start planning their next overseas trip, new life quest, and definitely, to book their next massage!"

—CHERIE KEPHART, AWARD-
WINNING AUTHOR of *A FEW MINOR
ADJUSTMENTS: A MEMOIR OF HEALING*

"A compulsively delicious treat! Mandy Urena has written a massage therapist tell-all that will take you on a fascinating trip around the world. Venture behind the lavender oil and scented candles, straight to the heart of an ancient healing art. Urena will make you laugh. She will make you cry. She will teach you more than you imagined possible and leave you desperate for a shiatsu massage. *Touchy, Feely, Squeezy* is so much fun, a must-read, and the perfect girlfriend gift!"

—HOLLY KAMMIER,
BEST-SELLING AUTHOR of *KINGSTON
COURT* and *CHASING HOPE*

"Funny and at times poignant, *TOUCHY, FEELY, SQUEEZY: MUSINGS OF A MASSEUSE* is an intriguing look at the people behind the hands that massage our aches away, as told by witty newcomer Urena."

—MIKEL WILSON,
AUTHOR of *MURDER ON THE LAKE OF FIRE*

"In this poignant and engaging memoir, Mandy Urena's sense of humor and heart shine. Through questioning and self-doubt, Mandy discovered that her passion for connection was not only a career but a vocation—the best of both worlds, in my estimation."

—CLAUDIA WHITSITT,
AWARD-WINNING AUTHOR
of *KIDS LIKE YOU* series

A COMICAL MEMOIR

Touchy, Feely, Squeezy

Musings of a Masseuse

MANDY URENA

Touchy, Feely, Squeezy: Musings of a Masseuse
First Edition

Cover design by Damonza

Book formatted by Damonza
http://www.damonza.com

ISBN: 978-1-947392-12-0

For Olivia Newton-John, my life-long idol and inspiration—a true angel to the world

Thanks to…

Orlando for loving me and supporting all my crazy ideas, including writing a book; Cheyenne, my beloved pup, for her unconditional love; my family in Coventry; Holly and Jess at Acorn Publishing for being my biggest fans and holding my hand; Southern California Writers' Conference (SCWC) for teaching me the craft; Pauline Turner, my high school English teacher who taught me how to write; Mrs. Atkin, my head mistress who tried to make a lady out of me; and Mum and Dad, Diane and Dennis Dumbleton, for putting me on this planet so I can travel this beautiful world and massage its beautiful people.

And a special thanks to my beta readers for critiquing my book: Carol Kirchner, Rich King, Stephanie Schulz, Nicola Hegarty-Hugh, Rebecca Gallardo, Louise Holyfield, Kate Dumbleton, Sharon Jensen, Karen Hemmet, Melissa Connelly, Louise Wyatt, Susan Walters-Peterson, Mary Conner, Cherie Kephart and Mikel Wilson, Sonia Bem and Claudia Whitsitt. And lastly, thanks to Eva Space and Tasha Hoglund for allowing me to read my book to them for Storytime. You believed in me from day one and set this literary ball rolling.

Contents

CHAPTER 1

Epiphany under a banyan tree in Thailand

"Turn off your mind, relax and float downstream…"

—John Lennon

I T ALL BEGAN on a beach in Thailand when I was asleep, and I almost missed it. I was on vacation trying to escape the stress of working three jobs and the hustle and bustle of life in Tokyo. With not a care in the world, nor a thought in my head, my plan was to do nothing but lie comatose with my feet in the surf.

But someone had other ideas.

"Lady! You want massaaaaa?" I was awakened from my deep slumber on Chaweng Beach, my tropical sunbathing interrupted by a tiny Thai lady with a not so tiny voice. Not wanting to be disturbed, I remained unresponsive, pretending not to hear. It worked because finally she went on her merry way.

But the next day, same thing—this persistent mini masseuse bellowing in my ear, her tone rising as she spoke: "Lady, you wan massAAAAAAAAAA? Is very good for you…"

This happened for three days in a row, until finally I stopped pretending to be asleep and let her rub me. In all my twenty years, I had never had a massage before so I had no idea what to expect, but friends raved about how heavenly massages made you feel, so curiosity got the better of me and I gave in.

The lady with her beaming toothless smile put down her tattered straw mat under the shade of the huge banyan tree next to me and motioned me to lie down on my belly. I adjusted my new hot-pink bikini which I had just purchased that morning on the beach because it perfectly matched my lipstick, and pushed my spikey blonde hair back into a band. My masseuse knelt on the soft white sand at my side and proceeded to rub me with oil—first my back, then legs and feet. Her touch was warm as she squeezed and rubbed and caressed my sore, tired muscles. I inhaled the aroma of the sweet coconut oil and soon started to doze back off to sleep. But it was only momentary, as I began to feel her walking on me–her feet pounding rhythmically on the back of my thighs, then her heels digging into my butt and the small of my back.

She was stomping on me and I was her human grape!

Unfazed, she proceeded to stretch me, pulling and pushing and twisting and bending my arms and legs. Still on my belly with her feet planted into the back of my thighs, she took ahold of both my arms, intertwining them with her own. Then she arched me into a back-bend, my face looking up to the sky. This was becoming more like a workout and I was thankful when she released my arms and put me down, so I was lying flat again. But my workout continued as she crossed my feet and pushed them towards my butt with the weight of her entire body.

I had gone from human grape to human pretzel and my afternoon nap on Koh Samui had turned into my very own contortionist act. This was not what I was expecting at all!

As unorthodox as this was, however, I did feel surprisingly good afterwards—the stretches seemed to send a surge of energy around my body; I could move, I could breathe and my stiffness and pain had done a disappearing act. The stress was gone and I felt new and improved—an updated model of my former self. This body-rubbing business was brilliant! So, when I heard that familiar high-pitched screeching in my ear, I simply had to take her up on her kind offer and gladly part with another ten dollars, the price of her magic.

It was there and then I had my epiphany, under the shade of a huge banyan tree—I wanted to learn how to do this, to perform magic too and make other people feel relaxed and stress-free.

And so, in the roasting sun, surrounded by tuk-tuks, temples, and sarong-clad women touting fresh lychee and mangosteen, on the island of Koh Samui in Thailand, began my two-decade love affair with massage.

Being pummeled and tied up into knots on the beach that day was my first step toward an unexpected life of massage therapy: a life of world travel, massaging rock stars, elite Navy Seals, cancer survivors, babies in the womb, and the sick and dying about to take their last breath—all sprinkled with an unfortunate handful of misbehaved fools who had a warped concept of the therapeutic intention of massage.

At twenty, my real life was just about to begin…

CHAPTER 2

Too cool for school

"There's no greater gift you can give or receive than to honor your calling. It's why you were born. And how you become most truly alive."

—Oprah Winfrey

*N*EVER IN MY life had I thought I would want to rub people for a living. Rubbing was not very academic and I was in the top of my class. I had always put massage into the same category as hairdressing and beauty and thought that girls at the bottom of the class who weren't very academic did "that sort of thing."

I attended an all-girls private boarding school in England, where I was born, and we wore matronly starched blue uniforms with straw boaters on our heads in the summer and blue bowler hats in the winter. It was all very posh. According to Mrs. Atkin, the headmistress, I was destined to do great things. She thought I should go to business college after high school which to me, being sixteen years old, sounded so desperately dull.

My dream was to work in America—as what, I neither knew

nor cared. I just knew that seeing America would be an adventure and I wanted some excitement in my life. All Brits fantasize about going to America at some point and I was no exception. I was lured by the sunshine and the beaches of Los Angeles, the glam of Hollywood, and the hustle and bustle of the Big Apple. It all seemed so grand and impressive and I dreamed of living and working in any one of those places one day, not sitting in a classroom reading more textbooks the size of doorsteps. Of course, I was alone with these ideas and plans: Mandy, wannabe globetrotter and international jet setter, party of ONE.

Neither my headmistress nor my parents were on board and they all conspired against me "for my own good," making me sign up for classes at the local college after high school. I felt defeated—my globetrotting ambitions had been squashed like a bug. But I just did not agree with being part of the rat race, which dictated that you go to school, then college, then get married, have two kids and two car payments, a mortgage, pay taxes, retire and die. It was a cookie-cutter lifestyle of which I wanted no part. Why couldn't I fly off to America and see the world?

I protested, but Mrs. Atkin had nothing more to say on the subject and my father fully supported her. To be fair, the one thing she did say that made sense and I have never forgotten (apart from, "Amanda! You will never make anything of yourself if you continue to fill your head with boys and discos!") was "Always have lots of hobbies and outside interests, because one day, they may be your bread and butter." Little did I know back then how true I would find her words to be.

As it went, the massage career that I never knew I wanted, turned out to be not only my bread and butter, but my steak and lobster too, followed by rich crème brulee topped with sweet Chantilly cream. *And* a maraschino cherry. I am just not a bread and butter kind of girl.

CHAPTER 3

Traditional Japanese shiatsu: made in China?

"Let food be thy medicine and medicine be thy food."

—Hippocrates

I MADE ALL THAT fantasizing about the USA a reality when I turned nineteen. After a little backpacking around Europe and a stint on a kibbutz in Israel, I met a Californian named Kip and followed him to L.A. I felt like I was in a movie with stretch limos cruising the huge boulevards, beach bars and bikini-clad babes with perfect bodies rollerblading on the promenade. I walked around, eyes and mouth wide open, marveling at everything I saw. Everything except Kip. So, without missing a beat, I moved on.

I rented a small apartment a block from the beach and zoomed around Hermosa on my scooter in my bikini; I was living the beach life in America. America! At nineteen years old, armed with my fake ID purchased for $60 from the intersection of Sunset and Vine, I hit up the bars, hung out with tanned surfers sporting long shorts and long hair, and learned how to do shots with names like Fuzzy Navel, Sex-on-the-Beach and Bloody Brain. I went out to breakfast at 2 a.m. and ate pancakes. L.A. life was mind-blowing to a Coventry girl—a far cry from starched uniforms and boarding school rules.

During the day, I worked in a stockbroker's office as one of those annoying cold-callers, hired solely on account of my British accent, and in the evenings, I was working as a cocktail waitress in a jazz bar serving food I had never heard of before, like guacamole, fajitas and jalapeños, none of which I could pronounce. We never ate those things in England when I was growing up, so when I asked my customers if they would like jappelinos on their pizza, they laughed, thought it was cute and gave me big tips!

I was certainly getting my fair share of culture, but a year of pancakes, shots, and surfer dudes was enough. The novelty of working in America wore off, and the appeal of dating surfers with long, messy hair waned. I had embraced their free spirits and rugged good looks at first, but after a while they lost their luster, and I just wanted to tell them to get a haircut and take a bath! Who knew that life in L.A. would get mundane so quickly? But what was I going to do next?

I knew I didn't want to go home to England; I still yearned to experience new cultures and adventure. So, I looked east. Far east. *The* Far East. Enticed by the Land of the Rising Sun, I called my Japanese friend from boarding school, Inji, who lived in Tokyo. At school, back in England, Inji and I had made a pact that I would visit her in Japan one day, and just like that, I decided that I was going to Tokyo to live.

My year's worth of waitressing tips and $5 an hour receptionist's pay added up. I arrived the day before New Year's Eve in 1988 with the grand total of $1,000, which was more money than I'd ever had in my life. The city was in full party mode.

Bright lights, tall buildings, millions of people with shiny black hair and Burberry raincoats. Crowded trains, exorbitant prices for everything, mind-boggling customs, and odd little idiosyncrasies. For many people, living in Tokyo takes some serious getting used to. But not for me: I loved it the second I arrived. It was all spectacular and such a novelty.

From the very first day, I threw myself into the culture, leaving no doubt in my mind that I must surely have been a Geisha girl in a past life. It was the Eighties, and blondes were in high demand for modeling jobs, TV and movie-extra roles, and even teaching English in any of the hundreds of English conversation schools dotted around the city. It seemed that blue eyes and blonde hair were the main criteria needed to be an English teacher in Japan—never mind if you had teaching qualifications or not. Green-eyed teachers were highly sought after too, and as I discovered, I also had a natural talent for teaching, so it appeared I was over-qualified. So, I did all those "blonde" jobs in the daytime and at night I worked in a karaoke bar.

Japan was booming, and there was an upsurge in jobs for "*gaijin*"—foreigners—for which workers were paid ridiculous amounts of money. I took them all. I had been there barely a year and I was making $5,000 a month juggling English grammar books, modelling gigs, TV studios, and movie sets. I didn't mind being a workaholic working fourteen hours a day because it meant that I could afford to dine in posh restaurants, buy designer clothes like Issey Miyake, and live the high life—a very different experience from my friends back in my hometown who were in college or working full-time in an office.

In Tokyo, I lived it up, and most of my *gaijin* friends did too. I think the Japanese government must have gotten wind of all the foreigners working illegally and raking in the yen, because they implemented a new law: foreigners could only remain in Japan on work visas if they studied "something cultural." It could be *Karate* (Japanese martial arts), *Ikebana* (the study of flower arranging), *Chanoyu* (the art of the tea ceremony), *Nihongo* (Japanese language), or *Shiatsu* (Japanese massage). I needed to enroll in something in order to stay in the country because, for me there was no going back.

My only experience with massage thus far had been under the banyan tree in Thailand the previous year on vacation, and I had enjoyed it so much that I decided I wanted to do it for a living. Now, here was my chance. So, rather than learning to stick daffodils in vases or chop planks of wood in half with my bare hands, I signed up for Japanese massage classes.

The shiatsu course was taught by an eccentric Australian from the Outback, so thankfully it was in English. His name was Bluey and although he looked like the typical tanned and rugged Aussie, he fancied himself a native and had adopted quirky little Japanese mannerisms. He was fully-immersed in the culture having lived with his Japanese wife in Tokyo for ten years, and he came to every class dressed in a Japanese kimono-like *happi* coat. His traditional indigo-blue coat featured the words Bluey-Sensei embroidered on the front—sensei being Japanese for teacher and showing deference, and that is how we were to address him at all times.

He held classes in his small Japanese home, and the students massaged each other in the living room on futon mats on his *tatami* straw-like floor. I might not have been so eager to sign up had I known I would be crawling around on all fours all day, but the saving grace was getting paired up with a six-foot-tall, tanned Swiss guy who had come to Japan to study karate. What a chore it was going to be to have to partner up with that Schwarzenegger-like body, week after week for an entire summer! But somehow, I knew I would manage, and from day one, I decided I quite liked shiatsu. The class was going to be great! Besides, I was going to learn something uniquely Japanese.

So, it was much to my disappointment when Bluey-Sensei was teaching us about the history of this Japanese art form and said, "Shiatsu isn't actually Japanese. In fact, it came from China in the 6th century."

What? Even shiatsu was made in China? Well that isn't very authentic at all; it's like ordering the spicy tuna sushi roll but being served crispy fried wontons instead. I have been duped!

"It was actually introduced to Japan by a Buddhist monk along with herbalism as part of traditional Chinese medicine. But over a period of five thousand years, the Japanese have adapted and modified it, making it their own."

Like with the automobile industry and electronics.

"In China, it was the blind people in the north who did the shiatsu. Unlike the land in the south of China, the North was barren and couldn't produce the herbs or oils needed to make the healing potions that were used in Chinese medicine. So, they had to come up with another method to heal the body naturally, and pressure point massage—shiatsu—was born."

Our *sensei* went on to explain that shiatsu was performed by blind people because they had a heightened sensitivity due to the loss of one of their five senses, and their sense of touch was naturally more acute.

As I pondered blind Chinese people giving massages in the barren lands of China, I couldn't help feeling that my cultural experience wasn't as Japanese as I had hoped. But then I looked around the class and snickered to myself. What was I moaning about? As far as experiences go, this couldn't be any more cultural or international. There I was, a Brit in Japan, studying what I thought was a native art, but was really Chinese, taught by an Australian, partnered up with a tasty Swiss beef-cake, and my classmates were from America, New Zealand, Sweden, Germany, Argentina and Kenya. It was like being at the United Nations.

As interesting as the history of shiatsu was, I was eager to get to the hands-on part of the class: hands on the beef-cake that was my partner. Hands on those plump rounded muscles of his. I really wanted to oil him up at this point and sink my fingers into his chest muscles, but it turned out, that's not what shiatsu is all about. As unorthodox as it may seem, recipients of this type of massage remain fully-clothed and there isn't a drop of oil in sight; it's all about the pressure.

During the practical classes, our teacher would call out

step-by-step instructions, and we would all massage together doing the same moves in unison. We started with our partners lying prone—face down—on the mat.

"Kneel at the side of your partner facing across their body, and with one hand on top of the other, palm along the far side of the spine applying even pressure from the shoulder to the buttocks. Next, using both thumbs, press along the ridge adjacent to the spine. Lean in, stimulate for five seconds and release. Then move to the next point about an inch down, again working your way from shoulder to buttocks. Stimulate, hold for five, and release."

It was a lot of leaning in and using our own body weight to apply the right amount of pressure. We used mainly our palms and thumbs to do the massaging until we reached the buttocks, and then we used our elbows. Shiatsu was easy enough to do apart from the crawling around on our knees.

It wasn't until we got down to the feet that we finally got a break and were able to stand up. I liked working on the feet because we literally got to stomp on our partners. We used our own feet to massage theirs with both our heels applying the pressure: stomp with the right foot, stomp with the left, rinse and repeat. We must have looked quite comical, as if we were trying to macerate our partners into a fine wine, but for the person receiving the stomping, it felt strangely comforting and relaxing.

After the guided instruction was over, we all sat on the floor with our note pads and learned the theory of our work. For most Westerners, the theory of Chinese medicine is an alien concept, so our Bluey-Sensei took it slowly. The first thing we learned was that the word shiatsu meant "finger pressure." Never mind that we were actually using our thumbs, elbows, knees and heels to do the massaging; it is the pressure of the finger after which this style of massage is named. I thought this was a little misleading but refrained from any smart comments.

Bluey-Sensei, dressed as usual in his indigo-blue *happi* coat, was sitting in traditional *seiza* position on his knees to teach the class. He asked, "How does everyone feel? Do your muscles feel relaxed? Are your neck muscles looser?" Everyone, although still half asleep, agreed that their muscles did indeed feel relaxed after the prodding, poking and stomping.

"What if I were to tell you that shiatsu has nothing to do with the muscles and that we are working with the energy circuits of the body? We are stimulating energy pathways called *meridians* rather than the muscles themselves."

He used the analogy of the body being a network of highways. When we are healthy, the energy flows effortlessly around the circuit, but when we are stressed—physically or emotionally—there is a pile up, a stagnation of energy and this is what causes illness. The stimulating of each pressure point along the meridians unblocks the trapped energy and sends it on its merry way around the circuit, bringing the body back into balance. It's like connecting the dots along the lines in a child's dot-to-dot drawing book.

I must have gotten the hang of it quite well because my Swiss partner seemed to be enjoying it and he dozed off a lot, his body melting under my hands like fondue. For him, it wasn't mandatory to study shiatsu as he was already in Japan on a student visa to study karate, but in between his martial arts and teaching German conversation, he wanted to learn how to massage too—just for fun.

He told me how he had started learning karate as a child and how he had come to Tokyo to master it. I hung on to his every word. Cute accent, beautiful face and a David-like sculpture for a body that, like Da Vinci's David, was larger than life. I wanted to gobble him up like Swiss chocolate, and I looked forward to each Wednesday afternoon when I would see him again.

In our next class, we focused primarily on the legs and it was my turn to be massaged first. As Beef Cake worked on my legs and thighs, I closed my eyes. Did someone mess with the thermostat because it was getting hot in here? Agghh, I wished I didn't have such a crush on him; it made it really hard to concentrate. Not that

I should have been concentrating; I should have been relaxing, but I will admit, I had a hard time keeping my thoughts clean. My impure daydreams were soon interrupted as our instructor came over to us and used my thighs as a teaching moment for the class.

"The meridians you are stimulating on the legs all correspond to different organs of the body. The meridian running down the middle of your quadriceps is the stomach meridian and running right along beside it on the inner thigh is the liver. In fact, you have now worked on all twelve meridians of the body starting from the bladder on the back, which we learned in the first class."

Although I appreciated the gift of knowledge our esteemed instructor was bestowing upon me, I kind of wished that he would go away and bother someone else; I'd been quite enjoying getting my liver meridian stimulated. But he went on.

"And the last thing we are going to learn today is that not only is there an organ which corresponds to the meridians; there are specific emotions associated with each one, too."

He explained that the liver meridian, for example, is associated with anger—so theoretically, pain along that particular pathway would indicate that the client may be having some anger issues—consciously or subconsciously. Much of the time, emotional problems like anger, resentment and jealousy are heavily disguised as physical problems such as tight legs, a stiff neck and back pain. If the client is open to the idea that emotional turmoil manifests into the physical body, then this awareness may be all that is needed to release the problem.

Shiatsu was like reading someone's palm! This was fascinating and my annoyance with my teacher for interrupting my massage subsided. Who knew that you could tell so much just from massaging a person's body and that massage could sort out your emotional problems too? That blew me away.

From that day forward, I learned to look at pain in a different light, and I became more aware of my body for the first time in my life. As a girl born in 1968 in England, no one had ever taught me this; my culture believed sickness was random and that chronic back pain was just a bit of rotten luck.

It had taken the class twelve Wednesday afternoons to become proficient in ninety-minute pressure point massages and understand the basics of the Eastern philosophy associated with shiatsu. Although I began studying out of necessity to renew my work visa, shiatsu had taught me so much about the culture and traditions of the country I was to call home for eight years. Japan was already under my skin.

In the capital city, there seemed to be a shiatsu parlor on every corner and Tokyoites scurried in and out from morning into the late evening for a quick tune-up on the body. A benefit of fully-clothed massage is that there's no messing about changing clothes or showering off oils. Shiatsu is a full-body makeover with the power to transform an exhausted Japanese salaryman on his last legs at lunchtime, into a fearless Samurai at his afternoon meeting. A one-hour session for $60—or even a half-hour session for $30— is a makeover which makes all manner of aches and pains suddenly disappear; a sure return on investment. It's Japanese wizardry!

It seems that the Japanese people weren't the only ones who believed in the power of shiatsu. Japanese government officials must have enjoyed its powers too, because in 1964, the art of shiatsu was officially acknowledged as a legitimate healing therapy in Japan.

Unfortunately, shiatsu isn't as popular in America or England as it is in Japan, but it is offered at spas all over both countries. Even though it might be on the menu, people seem to be reluctant to try it because they are unsure exactly what to expect and the word pressure tends to conjure up images of steamrollers and grimacing pain. Besides, it is difficult for Westerners to imagine how a fully-clothed massage would feel relaxing and even more confusing to try and understand the principles behind it. Thankfully, it isn't necessary to understand its principles for it to feel good, and I would go as far as to say that a technical explanation would send a potential client running for the exit.

"Now then, Mrs. Higginbottom, I am going to massage your meridians today and stimulate the energy in your kidneys. And then I will unblock the anger in your liver meridian."

Not only does the description sound terrifying, it doesn't sound very spa-like at all. Or very Zen. Explained simply as a "pressure point massage which helps rebalance the body's energy" would do the trick. Boom! Sold! That's much more Zen and who doesn't need a little rebalancing?

Since my introduction to shiatsu back in the Eighties, I have given and received countless sessions and I remain a big proponent. Little did I know back then that the seed planted in Thailand would be fed and watered in Tokyo and that this class would catapult my career and become my life's passion.

Talking of passion, three years later I bumped into the side of beef that was my massage partner on the streets of Tokyo quite by chance, and unrequited lust turned into a long overdue summer fling.

A few years after that, he became the karate champion of Europe and opened a karate school in Switzerland! Turns out our time in Japan was good for both of us.

CHAPTER 4

Building a repertoire in Germany

"Too often we underestimate the power of a touch, a smile, a kind word; a listening ear, an honest compliment, or the smallest act of caring, all of which have the potential to turn a life around."

—"Dr. Love," Leo Buscaglia

A FEW YEARS LATER in 1996, armed with my shiatsu training and a new accessory to my name, I moved from Japan to Germany. My latest attachment was an American G.I., an Air Force guy who made a very cute arm charm and who I finally married after a year of saying "Don't be ridiculous! I don't believe in marriage. Go and sow some wild oats for goodness sake!" I have always thought marriage a very foolish notion and statistically speaking, a bit of a failure. All you have is a fifty/fifty shot at best and what's worse is you already know the numbers going in; it's a flip of a coin whether it's going to be bliss or bust, so it's not much of a safe bet.

And so, I was on my soap box for months, reeling off countless reasons as to exactly why I thought marriage was so ridiculous, when one day I thought about it long and hard: Orlando was a wonderful guy, loving and kind, and we always had fun together. Besides, he had big brown eyes and a nice bum. Looking into his eyes over warm apple pie à la mode late one Sunday evening I said matter-of-factly, "Alright, I give in. I will marry you." Just like that, out of the blue. Real romantic! Shortly afterwards, the U.S. military stationed us in Ramstein, Germany and it was goodbye, Asia…hello, Europe and a whole new life ahead.

I had no idea how I was going to get a massage job in Germany, as I didn't speak the language. But I wasn't going to let that hold me back. I thought my best bet would be to ask at the gym on Ramstein Air Force Base because it was a NATO base shared by Americans, Canadians, and Brits, and they all spoke English. At the gym, I found the manager and told him I was interested in doing massages and that I had studied shiatsu in Japan. The look on this clean-shaven preppy manager in his sensible khaki pants and freshly-ironed golf shirt told me he didn't know what shiatsu was. A better explanation was in order.

I elaborated, "It's a Japanese style pressure-point massage that you usually do fully-clothed."

"Fully-clothed?" He cocked his head, his contorted expression letting me know I was not selling this well and I might as well be speaking Swahili. I suppose "clothed pressure massage" doesn't sound very sexy, and so I did the next best thing and offered him a free massage. When in doubt, offer the freebie; it works every time! Just as I hoped, his interest piqued and we talked further as he led the way to the massage room.

After asking the preliminary health questions, I instructed him to get up on the table exactly as he was, wearing his pants and shirt. There was already a disc in the CD player, and so I pressed play to create the mood, turned the lights down and covered him for warmth with the soft fluffy blanket already at the foot of the table. I worked on him for about 40 minutes, stimulating the pressure points, squeezing and stretching. By the time I turned him over he looked wiped out and hazy—total relaxation.

I finished the interview massage by rubbing the pressure points on his head and face, gave a little tug of the hair, and I do believe I had my first convert because he said, "I never want an oil massage again after this Shitzu thing." I laughed to myself. I didn't have the heart to correct him or explain the obvious difference between a squashed-faced little dog and a Japanese massage, because he hired me right there on the spot.

He gave me two days a week to start and I was to share the job with another part-time therapist who worked there. Job sharing was fine by me for my first job in the field because I wasn't sure just how many massages I could physically do in one day.

I was excited that I was going to be a professional and actually get paid for doing what I loved to do, but I couldn't help thinking that this wasn't my master plan. I always thought I would have a big international corporate job like many of my friends back home. I knew what they thought of me doing massage for a living; they thought I had wasted my education and should be doing something more intellectual. Maybe they were right, and there were times when this thought plagued me. But this was my first job in the field and it wasn't forever. I had plenty of time before I settled down into a full-time, full-on career. But for now, I was focused on my new job at the gym.

The first week I looked at the schedule and noticed the other therapist who did Swedish oil massages was booked solid on Monday, Wednesday and Friday. I supposed that was understandable because most people didn't know any other style so by default, they requested a regular relaxing massage, known as Swedish. In contrast to my colleague's packed schedule, I had hardly anyone on my days.

The forecast for the second week was just as dismal with only a couple of bookings, while she was booked out at least three weeks in advance with a waiting list the length of the Great Wall of China. Fortunately for me, some people were so desperately in need of bodywork they signed up with me as a last resort, out of defeat. I was second best; I was the red-headed step-child of massage therapy and my ego was punctured and deflated, lying in a heap on the floor.

The word on the street was that if you wanted a massage within the next month, you had no choice but to opt for shiatsu with Mandy. At least I had *some* clients—no matter that they were the misfits—the desperate people with unmanageable aches and pains, the people who had slept funny and couldn't turn their heads, and the last-minute bookings bought as an anniversary gift from frantic husbands who had forgotten what day it was. But thanks to this motley crew, word of mouth spread that even though shiatsu was quite different from Swedish, it was different in a really good way, if not better.

Week by week, more and more people tried it and loved it, re-booked appointments, and told their friends. My new clients walked out feeling like their bodies had gone through a full-service tune-up. My work had delivered, as promised. Soon, I was seeing four or five people per day, and picked up another day of work. The money started rolling in. Even some of the diehard Swedish fans who didn't want to try a different technique at first, came around because the alternative was having to wait.

My headmistress was right; my hobby had become my bread and butter—*meine brot und fett*, as they say in Germany. Well, I couldn't be sure if they actually did say that, because my German language skills remained only food-based. I never did embrace the complicated masculine, feminine and neuter grammar rules of German which dictate that a potato is feminine, but a sausage is gender-neutral.

After a few months of doing five shiatsus per day, I decided I wanted to learn more about my new career field and all its different modalities. As luck would have it, I found a school a couple of hours away. OK, it was in England and I was in Germany so technically it *was* only a couple of hours away, albeit by plane.

It was a beauty school that taught massage, facials and cosmetology, and students could come to the school on their own schedule and do all of their theory and practical case studies at home. So, I studied massage and facials and juggled my schedule going back and forth every month or so to England for a week of beauty school.

Beauty school! I couldn't help but think of Frenchie in the movie *Grease* with pink hair singing *Beauty School Dropout* with Frankie Avalon. Even though the mental image made me giggle, I was afraid that people would think I was like her, only doing massage because I didn't have the intelligence to do anything else. Was there still this stigma? I put this gnawing, self-defeating thought aside.

I enjoyed learning anatomy and physiology and all about the skin, and six months later I passed my exams with honors. This meant I was certified under *ITEC*—a Europe-wide governing body—to do Swedish massage, the oh-so popular Monday, Wednesday and Friday massages.

Back in Germany I was eager to add my newly-acquired skills to my, as yet, small repertoire, and offer both shiatsu and Swedish to my clients at the gym. My boss was only too happy to offer more choices to our clients, but it meant competition for my fellow massage therapist. She got her knickers in a twist and whined and plotted against me saying I wasn't qualified in the U.S, which was perfectly true because my school was in England. But we weren't in the U.S.; we were on an international NATO base on German soil, so my qualifications were indeed valid. I wanted to say, "You're not in Kansas anymore Dorothy!" The nerve of her!

Despite the petty squabbling and sabotage attempts, I managed to build up a large clientele and quite a good reputation in my first year. However, I decided that job sharing with Dorothy was underwhelming so I left the gym, started my own mini practice in the back of my house, and took all my clients with me. And a few of hers too!

It was great being self-employed in a small military community. The base even had its own newspaper where I could advertise, and since the entire community picked up this free weekly paper, it was easy to market myself and my new enterprise which I named *The Pressure Point*. Even if I do say so myself, I thought it to be a very clever name considering my shiatsu training. Advertising was easy and I booked a steady stream of new clients each time my ad came out on Fridays.

Despite the effectiveness of my newspaper ad, I much preferred to receive new clients by word of mouth because a referral usually meant a more trustworthy person would be coming through my door. When new clients hadn't been referred, I devised a system to protect myself the best I could in an effort to weed out any miscreants. I vetted new people on the phone by asking medical questions like, "Did your doctor refer you? What kind of pain are you in? Are you experiencing sciatica, a frozen shoulder, fibromyalgia?" This usually worked, and if there happened to be a depraved character at the other end of the line thinking my massage practice was *Happy Endings R Us,* he would usually hang up when I put on my nurse hat and threw down big medical words.

I took as many precautionary measures as possible, but often times as I really didn't know who was coming through my front door, I pulled this little stunt. To make people think my husband was home, I would whisper as I opened the front door and say, "Sshhh, my husband is sleeping so we need to be quiet walking up the stairs." Or I would simply put the TV on loudly in the living room hoping they would naturally assume someone was home, and I would say, "I will leave you to get undressed and I will go and tell my husband to turn that TV down. He must be deaf!" And that would make me feel safe even though I was alone in the house.

There weren't many other people doing massage in the small

German communities around the base apart from Dorothy and one other therapist, Anne-Marie, so we had a monopoly on massages in the area. If you wanted a good massage outside the gym, you either came to me or to Anne-Marie, and there was enough business for the pair of us. Soon I had regular clients and a good reputation. I had come far from the red-headed stepchild zone.

My knowledge of the industry, along with my repertoire, was expanding, yet still I wanted to learn more. I liked the idea of studying the ancient Egyptian art of foot reflexology because I had read that massaging the foot could heal the whole body. As luck would have it, I found another school in England—this time in London. And this time it wasn't beauty school; it was the Central London School of Reflexology which to me sounded a lot more professional and less girly.

I think, subconsciously, I was choosing schools in England, because as a Brit living in Germany, I was missing my family and all of my favorite comfort foods. By studying reflexology at home in England once a month for a year, I was feeding both belly and brain. I could jump on a train from London and arrive at home in Coventry in one hour. I dined on home-cooked Sunday roasts at the family dinner table, or feasted on take-away fish and chips from the local chip shop. There was even time for a pint in the pub with my childhood friends.

In between my feedings and trips to the pub, I did actually learn how to do reflexology. My school in Covent Garden in London was fun, and just like beauty school, we were required to do the theory homework in between classes and conduct ten case studies at home to get certified. During class, we exchanged treatments with our fellow students, and while half the class was following the protocol of the anatomy points on the foot, the rest of the class whose feet we were treating, dozed off.

The premise of reflexology is that all points on the foot correspond to—or are the reflection of—organs and systems of the body, and we can stimulate any body part through the foot. If someone has a headache, we stimulate points on the big toe without ever having to touch the head and miraculously the headache disappears. Similarly, if someone has a problem with weak kidneys, we prod and pinch and rub and twist the kidney reflex on the sole of the foot and that pushes out all the toxins, bringing the organ back into balance. It was amazing!

Back home at the base in Germany, I had my case studies to do and I recruited two of my friends. Ingrid was my Belgian client who I affectionately called Frenchie because she donned designer clothes, spoke French, and always wore French perfume, so she humored me. The first time I met her she had come to me in tears with chronic shoulder and neck pain due to her job as a cosmetics representative, a job that required travel all over Europe.

Ingrid was positively beautiful, like a supermodel. She didn't mind me calling her Frenchie, but she did mind being called a supermodel because she didn't see herself that way at all. But she absolutely was. She was tall with shiny chocolate hair, long tanned legs and perfect skin. And the highest cheekbones I have ever seen.

She started getting weekly massages and it became evident that the stress of days on the road, away from home, were physically and mentally taking their toll. She was unhappy in her job and as a result, her anxiety and stress had manifested in her physical body as neck pain, stiff shoulders, stomach ulcers and problems doing a "number two."

Embarrassed, she asked me if I could help her with the latter problem because she hadn't "been" in over a week—she was so conservative. I suggested she come more regularly as my case study. She agreed and so I began massaging her feet every day after work for five days. I focused on stimulating the digestive tract especially her colon but I did the whole hour protocol to help with her stress levels, too. It seemed to work because she fell asleep each time.

I couldn't help but notice how pretty Ingrid's feet were—beautifully pedicured, and they always smelled of roses. I think she sprayed them with rose water right before her appointment and I always made fun of her, saying I'd never met anyone with such rosy feet. Her husband loved to respond with "Don't be fooled. Her feet don't always smell of roses" and she would playfully slap him.

I also recruited Lynn to be my case study. She was my neighbor, a Southern Belle with bleached blonde hair and a knockout smile, who wanted to try reflexology to see if it would help with regulating her periods. That was a tall order and the only plan of action I had was to stimulate the areas around her ankle bones which corresponded to the uterus and the ovaries, and I thumbed along the tops of her feet which represented the fallopian tubes. I massaged fairly vigorously and hoped it would work.

With practice, I became more familiar with the techniques and more confident, and apparently, I was doing the right thing. I don't mean to be indelicate, but it only took two sessions for Ingrid to shit for Belgium, and just one session before my Southern Belle reported that she was bleeding like a stuck pig. But I wasn't quite sure if I should have been proud of that.

During that time in the late Nineties, I read about another new popular style of massage called La Stone or simply hot stone. It was all the rage in the U.S. Massage therapists were using heated smooth black basalt stones of all different shapes and sizes, from flat and thin for sliding under the shoulder blades, to finger shaped stones for sliding down the neck. The idea was to use the stones to knead the muscles, allowing the hardness of the stone and the heat to do the work. It was touted as a luxury spa treatment and cost much more than regular modalities, but it also had plenty of healing benefits.

As luck would have it, England had caught on too and there was a week-long study coming up near Coventry for certified professionals in the field. Excited at the thought of a nice roast beef and Yorkshire pudding at home and a pint of cider at the pub—got to get my priorities right!—I booked myself into this hot stone class.

It seemed like it would be easy to learn, and in a way, it was.

The new modality was much like Swedish using oils, except with hot stones in our hands. I liked that there was a lot of autonomy to this technique; no one was trying to put me in a box and there were no hard and fast rules or protocol to follow. But there was a very thin line between a good and a bad hot stone massage; one false move or moving too slowly could burn the client. Or worse, burn myself!

The trick to not burning the flesh was to flip the stones over and over in the hands whilst working on the body—it had to be done fast to disperse the heat. Another challenge was to not burn my hands getting the heated stones out of the very hot water, and to mitigate such happenings, our resourceful teacher suggested using mesh laundry bags to lift the stones out—just like the kind people buy at the supermarket to wash their dirty smalls on wash day. Whatever works!

We were also taught how to incorporate cold marble stones which had to be stored on ice, and this alternate hot and cold therapy was called La Stone—a little bit more up-market than hot stone alone. It was a juggling act using hot, then cold, then even hotter stones, then ice cold marble stones again.

If the flipping of the stones was fast enough and done skillfully, the clients couldn't tell the difference between hot and cold. For them, it was invigorating and relaxing at the same time: huge heated flat stones were resting on their stomach; rocks the size and shape of avocados were resting in their hands, and ice-cold marble stones were massaging their face. It was vascular gymnastics as the body's blood vessels dilated, constricted, and then dilated again, leaving clients in a state of total relaxation. It was a bit messy and I had to focus, but I liked it and it was a best-seller. Stone massage was fast becoming the new "in thing" in spas around the world.

After the class, my husband and I did a little weekend getaway to the medieval walled city of Bratislava in Slovakia. As with any new city we visit, we like to sample the culinary delights and the wine—first things first—then do a tour of the city by bus, boat or bicycle and look for a place to get a massage.

Turning down a tiny cobbled street of this post-communist town, we saw a sign outside a little storefront saying "masaz" with an arrow pointing downstairs.

"Did we strike gold? Is this what we think it is?" my husband asked.

"It has to be."

We followed the arrow hoping that "masaz" did indeed mean massage, and not some illegal drug hangout.

Thai orchids and the scent of lemongrass told us that we had entered a Thai spa and posters on the wall indicated that they offered both traditional Thai and also hot stone treatments. We were a little disappointed they didn't offer any typical Slovakian-style massages but, after my recent training in England, I was just as excited to try my first professional hot stone massage.

As instructed, I showered and donned the white linen Thai spa robe provided in the changing rooms. These robes were stylish, light and airy, and felt like they would be comfortable enough to lounge around in all day with a good book and a nice cup of tea. In my robe, I was ushered into the dim, candlelit room, told to undress and lie on the floor on the traditional Thai mat. The pretty young Thai girl with a Frangipani white flower in her hair, bowed before she started, then oiled me up and began massaging with the warmed-up lava stones. I was in for a treat.

Or so I thought.

The stones were a bit hotter than I was expecting. In class, we had learned about the perils of temperamental heating units so if the water was scalding hot, we either had to add cold water immediately, or flip the stones in our own hands until they cooled down. Somehow, I don't think my therapist got that flipping memo.

I was already tired after my traditional lunch of pork in heavy sauce and thick noodles, so I must have dozed off right away. On the verge of sleep in my alpha state, I was enjoying the warmth of the stones on my lower back. Then suddenly I screamed.

"Aghh! That's scorching hot!" I squealed like a little pig and bolted upright. Was she trying to boil my kidneys?

She rested on her knees fidgeting and looking down as if she was embarrassed as I sat there disgruntled, rubbing my boiled back. Reluctantly, I lay back down and let her continue with the legs. Maybe, like me, she was new to incorporating hot stones. Maybe she was nervous, maybe she would do better on my legs. Maybe…

"Aghhhhhhhh!"

She scorched me again! This time her butterfingers had dropped the stone between the top of my thighs and she was attempting to fish it out, burning my butt cheek in the process!

"For the love of God!"

I jumped up and stood naked, with my hands over the newly charred red patch on the back of my thigh, which I am sure matched the one on my kidney. The young girl sputtered another apology, but could surely see that my disgruntlement had escalated exponentially. I still had at least another 45 minutes left of my massage time, so I asked her to put the stones away—far away— and just give me a regular oil massage. For the next ten minutes, I remained on high alert but, not being able to relax at all, I decided to cut my losses and abort the mission.

Still in my robe, I marched to reception to inform them that I only had half a hot stone massage, and that my masseuse had badly burnt my bottom. The Thai receptionist didn't speak much English and I didn't speak a word of Thai or Slovakian.

"Must pay," she said.

"What? That's outrageous!" I screamed. "Even more outra-geous than the outrageous massage itself!"

Blank look.

"Must pay, lady."

I handed over the money and stormed back into the chang-ing room. I was huffing and puffing, down almost 50 bucks and nothing to show for it but two burns that looked like I had been pelted with tomatoes. Most attractive! I took off my robe and threw it on the floor in a tantrum.

If I am going to have to pay $50 for my war wounds, they should at least come with a free spa robe.

So, without further ado, said robe went straight into my bag and I hurriedly exited the premises with my loot, not waiting for my husband. Was that bad? Never mind; it was a rhetorical question.

In school, we were taught the importance of keeping the customer happy. Well, on that day, I was the customer, and that robe made me very happy so, theoretically, it was totally by the book: burglary justified.

Back in Germany, I used the robe for my clients who were getting facials.

"Ooh, what an exquisite robe! So stylish and comfy!" my afternoon client remarked. "Wherever did you get this?"

"Bratislava," I smiled.

With my new robe, new certifications and new treatments to offer, I was thoroughly enjoying running my own massage practice and, to my pleasant surprise, it was successful. I loved to touch people and see them renewed. My work was never boring, especially since I was offering Swedish, facials, reflexology, and now, hot stone. And to think I had always made fun of the girls at school who wanted to do hair, beauty and anything that fell under the umbrella of "that sort of thing!"

I was now in the same club. Ouch! That backfired. That tiny voice still niggled in my not-so-subconscious. *Shouldn't a privately-educated girl who wore a bowler hat from Dickens and Jones of London have a more academic career?*

Probably. And one day I would for sure because this was only a temporary dream I was fulfilling. For the short-term, I would focus on adding to my repertoire.

A few of my regulars had formed a collective that met every week to do group meditation and exchange ideas about self-awareness, and they invited me along. We talked about different healing massages like reflexology, aromatherapy, and reiki energy massage, which I knew nothing about. I knew nothing about meditation either.

"I just don't get meditation," I commented. "Isn't it the most boring thing ever to sit still and do nothing but listen to your own breath?" Everyone laughed. "You'll see," they said.

After a few sessions, I did see. I decided that all the meditation malarkey was, in fact, quite good. It was OK to doze off and day-dream. Not only was it OK, that was the whole point!

One week there was talk of a four-day retreat in Holland to learn Healing Touch massage, which nurses were doing in hospitals there and in the U.S, too. It was hailed as a light and subtle therapy and worked with energy. Light and subtle really wasn't my thing; this Taurean bull had never been known for her subtlety! But everyone was going and I had never been to Holland before so, excited to see some windmills, and maybe some tulips in Amsterdam, I joined them for the weekend course.

It was there in Holland that I learned about auras and how to feel the electric sizzling that is our body's energy. Feeling energy was a bit like holding an invisible bouncy ball between my two hands. As I moved them in and out, there was an almost prickly resistance; I was kneading invisible dough! What amazed me even more was when my partner swept my aura to massage away negative energy, I could feel her touch six inches away in my bubble, my own electromagnetic energy field.

Yes, it was certainly a little weird, but the end result was a feeling of complete peace and serenity, as if I had been healed. An additional bonus was the disappearance of headaches and back pain. And my partner didn't really "do" anything—nothing I could really put my finger on, anyway.

Who knew that this bull would embrace the subtlety of healing? I only got into massage therapy because I liked rubbing people and wanted to make them feel like the Thai lady made me feel under the banyan tree on Koh Samui; I hadn't been interested in other types of massage and didn't expect for one minute that I was going to learn about energy and auras or that the words massage and healing were, in fact, interchangeable. Being a part of that spiritual group opened my eyes to a whole new world of all-things-massage and all that fell under its umbrella.

When I returned from England and Holland, I started working on redesigning my brochures and price lists to add my newly acquired skills. It was such fun sitting down and writing whatever I wanted to write to describe each treatment. Besides being creative and making me feel entrepreneurial, the information would educate my clients, and give them options to try different types of massage. It was also a great way to increase sales and up-sell. I look back now at my original brochure and the prices of my treatments; they were a steal!

I was proud of my brochure and all five options I was able to offer my clients: shiatsu, Swedish, reflexology, hot stone and Healing Touch. I printed up hundreds of copies to distribute around the community. My creative juices were flowing, and my job was fun. I could work the days and hours I wanted, go on vacation when I wanted, take a day off whenever I liked, select my own clientele, create all my own ads, and design my own massage room. I was making my clients feel like a million dollars and only charging them $40—massage therapy was a great job! Of course, it was only temporary while we were in Germany. I was an intellectual, an academic—a multi-lingual academic at that—and I aspired to be more than just a masseuse one day. Like my friends, I was going to get a proper job at some point…

CHAPTER 5

Job description: masseuse, shrink, yenta

"I've learned that every day you should reach out and touch someone. People love a warm hug or just a friendly pat on the back."

—Maya Angelou

As I PONDERED getting a "proper job," my business grew. Exponentially. And it was in great part thanks to my friend and fellow therapist, Anne-Marie. She was leaving Germany, moving back home to America, and sending all her clients to me. All of them! She literally gave every one of her clients my phone number, highly recommending me and warned me, "You have no idea how busy you are going to be."

It wasn't until her regulars sat down with me with their schedules and booked their weekly standing appointments that I realized what she was trying to say. There was Jan every Friday at 3:30 p.m.; Paula every Thursday at 4 p.m. and Duncan every Wednesday and Friday morning at 8 am. I couldn't believe how swamped I had become!

I had gone from being the last resort to the flavor of the month, and everyone wanted a scoop of me! By 9 p.m. after my last client, I would slump on the couch and fall asleep within minutes with my cats, Phyllis and Florence, perched on my chest snoring along with me. Some days were easy and I would do a deep tissue followed by an aromatherapy facial, then a couple of relaxing Swedish massages and maybe a sit-down reflexology at the end of the day. That kind of schedule gave my achy hands a break. But if I had four or five deep tissue massages back-to-back—literally!—working on big, burly men, my back would ache and I would hobble like an old woman to the comfort of my couch after the last client left. Those kinds of days demanded a gin and tonic reward, and my husband was my built-in bartender.

Phyllis and Flo played an integral role in my business and were the only staff I had—not to mention, the only ones I could afford! Phyllis, a fat, scruffy mess of white, beige and black fur with a Maine Coon-like bushy tail, was mischievous and demanding and whined at my massage door to get my attention. Flo, by contrast, was a sleek grey and black striped tabby, the epitome of a shy, scaredy-cat. They were sisters, abandoned at only a few weeks old.

They had showed up on my doorstep one crisp fall afternoon and housed themselves permanently in my pot full of dead plants beside our heavy German front door. I liked to think that they chose me to be their new owner and after a few weeks, a few arguments with my husband, and a few tears and pleas of "I have grown to love these kitties and you are being mean," we kept them.

Phyllis and Flo became my welcoming committee and when they saw clients parking on the street they would run up to the car, meow loudly and escort them to the entrance. When I opened the door, I would see my clients plus one or two kitties on the doorstep, waiting to come in. My adopted felines were people cats.

One afternoon, sometime in early May, I was sitting giving a lady a relaxing aromatherapy facial with the door ajar just a tiny bit. Phyllis pushed the door open with her scruffy fat white face and leaped onto the massage table, nestling herself in between my client's knees. This wasn't my usual protocol and I stood up to throw my naughty kitty out. But my cat-loving lady stroked Phyllis's head and insisted on her staying. For the remainder of the hour, Phyllis lay curled up in a ball, purring and looking just as sweet as she could be. I should have charged extra for AAT: Animal Assisted Therapy. It's a massage thing, honestly.

Just as I had grown attached to my felines, I was becoming attached to my clients, too. It is only human nature to bond when you massage and nurture the same bodies on a regular basis, and it was hard to maintain a solely professional relationship with my regulars—not that I wanted to, but that's what we were taught in school. I didn't agree with that philosophy at all—not if you had an ounce of personality. People saw me not only as their massage therapist but as their friend, their doctor and their psychologist. It didn't matter how many times I quoted word for word from our school text book "massage therapy isn't a substitute for proper medical care," they still would rather have paid me than their co-pay at the hospital.

Week after week, my clients shared their stories, and I swear some of them thought they were getting a two-for-one massage therapist slash psychotherapist when they booked their appointments. Some loved to overshare, rendering me privy to their secrets, the intricate details of their love-lives, and the local juicy gossip. Sometimes it was better than a seat in the front row of the theater. Other things I wished I could un-hear.

Massage school prepared me to be a massage therapist, not the kind of therapist whose clients lay on a chaise longue pouring out their problems, and it certainly hadn't prepared me for being their stand-in doctor either. But astonishingly, people trusted me with their bodies and their personal problems more than they trusted their often-detached doctors. Clients assumed quite mistakenly that I knew about every ailment and disease on the planet. They would talk about their fibromyalgia and their endometriosis and sometimes when I had no clue what they were talking about, I would simply have to ask, "Tell me Mrs. Bartholomew, what exactly are the symptoms of your (insert name of strange disease) and what did your physician advise?"

Then they would reel off their symptoms one by one, saving me from looking like a dummy, and winning me major brownie points for appearing so knowledgeable about the disease—"appearing" being the operative word. According to the Code of Ethics, I was supposed to throw out the disclaimer saying that this is outside my scope of practice and as I am not a medical professional, I cannot diagnose. But I would simply say, "I am not a doctor but that sounds like (insert name of disease)." And they listened to me.

Business continued to grow and being my own boss meant I could take a vacation whenever my husband had leave from the Air Force. But the downside to being able to make my own schedule was that if I didn't work, I didn't get paid. Two weeks in Italy consuming copious amounts of pasta and Pinot Grigio meant zero dollars, and being sick in bed with flu, meant two or three days off multiplied by zero dollars. But even when I was as sick as a dog, my clients didn't like it.

In the winter of 1998 just approaching Christmas, I was so stuffed up with cold I couldn't possibly work. My throat was sore, I had lost my voice, and my nose was running like Niagara Falls. I called my client, who was also a very close friend, to cancel. Over the phone she must have been able to hear how sick I was, and I told her I had no choice but to reschedule her for fear of getting her sick, too. But to my surprise, she begged and pleaded for me not to cancel insisting, "I don't care if you give me the flu. I have been so looking forward to my facial and massage and I don't have another day off for weeks, I'm so swamped at work. Please don't cancel…pleeeeeeease!" At this point I threw my hands up and said to myself, "the customer is always right" and went to warm up the room.

I chugged down decongestant medicine, popped a cough-drop

in my mouth, applied a bit of lipstick, and pressed on with pride. Boxes of tissues served as my saving grace. Tucked away at the bottom of the bed, I surreptitiously placed a box in between my client's festively pedicured feet and another clutch of tissues at the head of the table. I worked for two hours uninterrupted, breathing through my mouth and sucking on cough drops as she lay relaxed, enjoying what was supposed to be her luxury spa treatment, which, from anyone else's standpoint, must have appeared anything but luxurious.

I was suffering, and my nose was dripping, so as I was doing her facial I had the genius notion of rolling up tissues, twisting them, and stuffing them up my nostrils with the ends hanging out. I changed them out every twenty minutes or so without her having any inkling of what I was doing, and I had my hand sanitizer right next to me. Not only was this highly unorthodox and unprofessional, it was gross and must have looked like a tasteless comedy sketch to any onlooker.

But what could I do? She had insisted. Fortunately, my client was oblivious and on her way out she claimed she was feeling "regal." It seemed unfair that the client left feeling like a queen while her massage therapist was left feeling like the drowned rat, belly-up in the castle moat. Months later, I told her about the tissues dangling from my nose and she thought it was absolutely hysterical.

It is not usually the massage therapist who does the nose dripping. No, in my experience it's usually the other way around. Some clients would be fast asleep with their mouths open, drooling unknowingly, and some would even drip snot from their noses onto my bare toes through the little face hole in the massage table. That was nothing compared to the culprits who farted unconsciously as they lay comfortably under their heavy blanket. Whoever said this massage business was glam?

Despite having bodily fluids dripping onto my feet and the occasional silent but deadly passing of gas, my new career was to my liking. I had a great reputation in the community as massage therapist, substitute doctor, and a shrink. And soon, quite unintentionally, I became known as a matchmaker, too!

I cannot say that I am not the meddling type because that would be lying; I absolutely am. But this was the first time I had played matchmaker and to my delight it paid off for two of my regular clients, Doug and Bettina. Doug had booked my three o'clock appointment and Bettina my four o'clock on the same day. So maybe it wasn't so much my meddling but fate itself?

Doug, a good-looking broad-shouldered pilot in the U.S. Air Force, sported sparkling green eyes and a beaming smile that showed off his perfect white teeth. He came in regularly, every two weeks when he wasn't flying. Doug was the kind of client who didn't say much and usually slept the whole way through.

With clients like this, work was relaxing for me and with the pan-flute music playing in the background and the sandalwood aroma of the candles, I could zone out; it was like I was massaging on auto-pilot. I loved this peaceful and calming work environment. Massaging calmed me down and balanced my normally energetic, fireball personality.

But this afternoon, there was to be no silence; Doug, all caffeined-up after a strong German coffee at lunch, was in the mood to talk. I asked how he was enjoying his tour at Ramstein Air Force Base and he replied that he kept busy going on skiing trips over the weekends to the Swiss Alps, but that he wanted a partner to share it all with; he was tired of being single and was looking for a girlfriend because it was "about time to settle down."

I said, "Well, what kind of women do you like? I will keep my ears open," and gave him a smile. I was joking and really thought nothing else of it. Until Bettina walked in for her four o'clock appointment. They must have crossed paths walking to and from their cars parked on the street.

Bettina was a tall, beautiful blonde with big blue eyes and cute dimples. She was a bright and bubbly teacher, who greeted me every week with a warm hug. Unlike Doug, she was not a napper and loved to chat during her massages. On this particular day, she walked through the front door, escorted by Phyllis. She wore a cute yellow flowery sundress showing her long athletic legs, but rather than acting like her chirpy self, she kept unusually quiet.

"OK, spill," I said.

"You're not going to believe my blind date last night. Can we say 'failure of epic proportions'? I am so mad!"

"Come on upstairs and tell me all about it."

Warm and comfortable under the blanket with a lavender heat pack on her neck, poor Bettina relayed the saga.

Her male coworker who she had taught with for five years had insisted she meet his friend. He just knew the two would hit it off and he hounded her until she finally gave in. But dinner was a disaster. Her date was an hour late, leaving her standing outside on the street in a short red dress feeling like a hooker.

When he finally showed up in a disheveled sports coat, he sported way too much facial hair. She could have forgiven the unwillingness to shave, but creamy Alfredo sauce stuck in his beard was a real turn-off. Maybe she could have even overlooked that until he asked the waitress to split the bill.

"And that's not even the worst part. He stays in his house every weekend playing video games. Oh, and he doesn't drink." She continued. "All I want is someone fun who likes to do active outdoorsy things—someone smart, funny. Oh, and not cheap! Is that too much to ask?"

Now my yenta wheels were turning and I blurted out, "I have someone for you!" She laughed until she realized I was serious. I told her about Doug, how handsome and smart he was, how he was always going skiing and how he liked good food and wine.

"He would be perfect for you!"

She wasn't at all convinced. So, after the massage I showed her a photo of him smiling his big smile in my husband's ski club magazine from a recent trip.

She took one look and immediately dismissed him. "His teeth look too big."

Orlando, eavesdropping from the other room, shouted, "Bettina, you're going on a date, not buying a horse!" After several more tries at convincing her how nice he was, she finally agreed to at least consider one, just one, blind date with my prize thoroughbred. I thought it only right to inform the horse himself, so I quickly called with the news that I may have found him a mare. I told him excitedly, "Doug, I have found you a wife!"

He laughed out loud at this and at the thought of a blind date, but with a what-have-I-got-to-lose attitude said, "Game on!"

Doug and Bettina went on a few dates and got on well. They shared the same sense of humor and the same taste in German wine; so far, so good. Bettina felt bad about the big horse teeth comment and conceded that he was indeed good-looking after all. So, here I was already patting myself on the back for my amazing new-found matchmaking skills when she called late one evening and said, "I thought we had a great time but he hasn't called me since then, and it's been two weeks."

No, this was not how it was supposed to go…what was wrong with him? I simply had to intervene—never mind if this was outside my scope of practice. Putting everything I had learned in ethics class aside, I called Doug under the pretense of asking if his back was feeling better. Without bothering to wait for his answer I asked, "Didn't you like Bettina?"

"Of course, I did," he said. "I just got back from flying a mission. I was planning to call her over the next few days."

So, my thoroughbred wasn't quite the racehorse I had betted on, but at least he was still running the race. Just a bit slow to take off. My perfect-for-each-other clients dated more regularly over the next few months and then things got serious when Bettina reported to me that he had said to her, "You rock." Shortly after, "you rock," turned into "I love you," and a few months after that they announced their engagement. Yay me! I did it!

The following year I was honored to be asked to make the speech at Doug's and Bettina's wedding and tell their guests about how they had met. My speech started off with, "You all know the reason why you are here and it's all because of one very special person: me!" And I told their story, much to everyone's joy.

The result of my meddling is that fourteen years later we still keep in touch and send Christmas cards even though we live on opposite sides of the world. Because of me and my massages, two people fell in love and created two more little people—a boy and a girl. And that may be one of my favorite professional accolades thus far.

CHAPTER 6

"What do you do if a guy gets a woody?" (and other unusual questions)

"I love a massage. I'd go every day if I could. I don't need to be wrapped in herbs like a salmon fillet, but I do love a massage."

—Jason Bateman

As a novice, everything about the massage industry was new to me, but my instructors had trained me well and I was prepared for many situations. There were also a few surprises along the way. For example, they did not warn me about having snot dripping on my bare toes through the face hole, nor did they teach me the step-by-step procedures for tactfully waking up a snoring client. And they failed to prepare me for the barrage of unusual questions that clients inevitably ask when they are on the massage table.

There seemed to be a series of common questions that everyone was curious about: Where do you get *your* massages? Do you have to go to school for this? What do you do for a living? Do people fall asleep? Do people snore? Do people fart? Does anyone ever get a woody? Now, I understand clients wanting to know who massages me, because I do massage all day long, so it seems logical that I would also need a massage at some point. This is a good question and I tell them that I trade with my peers. But I must say that some of the other questions stumped me.

When people are relaxing on the massage table, it's hard for me to understand their need to ask, "Did you have to go to school for this?" Surely, they are being facetious. I mean if someone just slaps on heaps of oil and wipes it around the body willy-nilly then they are probably untrained and can't tell a muscle from a grilled cheese sandwich, and so, no, they did not go to school for massage therapy. But when you're getting a damn good massage and the therapist focuses on muscles, incorporates stretches, and fixes your pain, it seems obvious that he or she does know what they are doing and must have learned those skills somewhere—like massage school. Such skill and knowledge don't automatically come with the body at birth.

And why do people think even for one nano-second that massage therapists are untrained? Is the general consensus, oh, the poor girl is probably not too bright and this is all she could do?

I have felt this to be the case on one occasion too many and it infuriated me. More importantly, those types of questions made me feel inferior. Why wasn't massage work more socially acceptable and respected? A good bodyworker has the knowledge, skills and the power to heal, to improve a client's posture, stress levels and well-being, but people still have preconceived notions about massage somehow being about sex or about it not being a legitimate area of study at college. It is ridiculous how it came to have such a bad rap. Dammit, I was going to make it my job to educate these ignoramuses!

In my defense, I wanted to reel off a long list of my qualifications and certifications, and shout out every accomplishment since kindergarten, but as of yet, I haven't *actually* done that. Why did I feel like I always had to defend myself and legitimize my chosen career field? Anyone who receives regular therapeutic massages knows that the work speaks for itself and is as valuable as any physical therapist or chiropractor. Do people ask *them* if they went to school?

Massage schools are big business. What many people don't realize is that tuition ranges from about $6,000 to $20,000 depending on the state, and the curriculum runs from six months to a year. Students have to learn the anatomy and physiology of the entire body, including the names of all the muscles—their origins, insertions and actions, as well as where all 206 bones of the body are located. This is crucial because bones are not soft tissue and are not to be massaged.

Massage by definition is "a systematic and scientific manipulation of the soft tissues of the body for the purpose of obtaining or maintaining health"—soft tissues are the operative words here and refer to muscles as opposed to bones, tendons, or ligaments. If you go to a random massage parlor with neon pink lights and feel like you're getting an elbow in your spine, it might be because the "therapist" has no clue about the skeletal system. In such places, which tend to be open all night, rumor has it the masseuses focus only on one "muscle" and they didn't have to go to school for that! In fact, masseuses don't have to go to massage school at all.

A masseuse never has to worry about taking exams on anatomy and physiology. She is simply a person who massages, and unfortunately the title has come to suggest a purveyor of happy endings in America. In Europe, it doesn't have that sexual connotation and according to the dictionary, the word "masseuse" is simply French for "a *female* who massages" and is even pronounced completely differently. If it is a male therapist, he is of course a "masseur" and therefore cannot possibly be a "masseuse." So, when people talk about their masseuse called John or Bruno, the mind boggles.

It is understandable how the general public gets confused between massage therapists and masseuses and people like to ask me what the difference is. I explain it like this. Massage therapists are the real deal. We have to go to school to learn not only about anatomy and physiology, but about diseases, business management skills, marketing and the Code of Ethics. And on top of all that theory, we have to physically practice daily massages on classmates and on the community before graduation.

Graduation from massage school only means that a person is certified; it doesn't mean that they are licensed. To get licensed in 2008, we had to pass the national boards exam, which is brutal, and has an astronomically high failure rate. I understand it was created in an effort to legitimize the practice, but we are massage therapists, not heart surgeons.

Personally, in a professional setting I always refer to myself as a massage *therapist* rather than a *masseuse* because I am more than just a female who massages. I have anatomy encyclopedias the size of doorsteps in my bookcase to prove it. That said, many of my clients do affectionately refer to me as their masseuse and I know they don't mean any disrespect by it, so I tend to overlook their blooper. In fact, I used the term for the title of this book because it sounded so much catchier, but I do know many professionals in the field who get bent right out of shape and will correct the linguistic blunder.

The "do you have to go to school for massage?" question, as annoying as it was, wasn't nearly as ridiculous as the question, "So what do you do for a living?" Such a question must surely fall into the "Stupid Question" category, especially when the person who asked was actually *on* my table getting a massage from me! Dumbfounded, one such conversation went like this:

Man with no neck and squinty eyes: "So, what do you actually do for a living?"

Me: "Well, obviously, I am a massage therapist. Obviously. I am here massaging you."

Still clueless man with no neck and squinty eyes: "But you

would only do a couple of massages here and there part time, so I was wondering what your real job is."

Defensively, I came back with: "I massage six, sometimes seven days a week and I average four to six people per day. I start as early as 8 a.m. and on a busy day I don't finish until after 9 p.m. This *is* my 'real' job and even if I wanted another one, there wouldn't be enough hours in the day. God only made 24."

My client smiled an awkward smile and finally stopped talking. But what baffled me was that he asked this question when he could see with his own two squinty eyes that I was indeed busy. Not only had it taken him a week to get in for an appointment, he saw the person before him leave. Would that not suggest a certain busy-ness? Nevertheless, he found it hard to grasp the concept that massage could possibly be a legitimate, lucrative full-time career. Maybe I should have answered, "Oh…apart from doing massages, I bake fancy cakes for a living—that is, when I am not grooming dogs and building houses." He might have been more appeased with that answer.

The "what do you do for a living?" question wasn't as common as some of the questions asked by clients before dozing off. I think they must have been embarrassed that they might be the first person in history to zonk out, and so they ask bashfully, "Do people ever fall asleep during massages?" or, "Do people snore?" I usually reply that indeed some do sleep and snore and that there are those clients whose lives are so busy with work and family that the *only* time they get to sleep restfully is when they are on the massage table. And then there are those at the very end of the sleep spectrum who are so exhausted that I have wondered, quite sincerely, if they might in fact be dead. Mac was one of those people.

Mac particularly enjoyed napping during his massages. He would even factor in his nap and say, "Let me sleep and wake me up ten minutes after you're done massaging me." Mac and his wife, Dee, used to come on Saturdays together. As one of them was getting worked on, the other would read downstairs and this was their

Saturday treat. One afternoon Dee didn't come, but as usual, Mac dozed off within the first few minutes of my hands touching his back. He snored loudly and when I said, "It's time to turn over now, Mac," he looked at me as if I had asked him to move a mountain. But he did as he was asked before falling back to sleep a split second later. He was still fast asleep by the time I finished the massage and, as he was my last client of the day, I thought I would leave him for an extra few minutes and I quietly tip-toed out.

As I was washing my hands in the bathroom the phone rang. It was my friend from England calling just to say a quick hello, but her quick hello turned into serious girly gossip which meant a nice cup of milky coffee was in order and so I went into the kitchen, still talking. An hour or more later, I was still on the phone when my husband popped his head around the door and asked what we were doing for dinner.

It was about dinner time, so I reluctantly stopped gossiping, put the phone down and thought about what to make. *Ooh, I know! Spaghetti Bolognaise! Haven't had that in a while.*

I began chopping and frying the onions and garlic, mixing in the ground beef and the tomatoes and spices and in less than 30 minutes, I had concocted a work of culinary genius even though I do say so myself. I dipped my finger in the sauce, *mmm tasty*! and started to set the table. I poured some wine and prepared to relax for the evening over a nice romantic candlelit meal for two, and maybe a movie afterwards.

Just as we sat down to eat, I heard a knock on the door. Annoyed that someone was interrupting my dinner, I slogged downstairs. There stood Mac's wife at my door. Her brow was furrowed, and her mouth rested in a tight line. She looked worried.

"I just came around to see if you knew where Mac was because he didn't come home after his massage appointment this afternoon."

Mac…oh no! Oh my God, I had forgotten Mac on the massage table! He must have been there for three hours or more and I had completely forgotten about him. Worried he might be dead, I sprinted upstairs to the massage room and there he was, still sleeping like a baby.

I felt awful about forgetting my client. Fortunately, he saw the funny side and so did Dee. My husband made fun of me for client neglect and Dee laughed at Mac because he could sleep for days if left to his own devices. The story of my client neglect went around the school where Dee and many of my clients worked, and while everyone thought it was hysterical, I never quite lived it down. To this day, I have never left any client for dead again. Well, that's not quite true; technically there was one.

Like Mac, Walt was also overtired and loved to sleep. I dare to say that his massage sessions were the only time he got to sleep undisturbed. Every appointment it was the same thing; as soon as Walt's head hit the face cradle and I'd tucked him under the heavy blanket, he would immediately pass out and start snoring within seconds. And loudly, at that. It was grunting actually, not unlike the sound that an overweight pot-bellied pig makes. His whole body would inflate on the in breath, and slump as he exhaled.

He was quite comical to watch, and I had to restrain myself from bursting out laughing. With Walt, I could have gone down to the pub for an hour, had a few pints and a ham sandwich, been back at the top of the hour, and he would have been none the wiser. But at the top of the hour, every week, it was like trying to wake the dead.

First, I would say quietly, "Walt, let's take a deep breath in to finish," just like I said to all my clients when their time was up. And then I would try again in a louder voice, "Walt, it's time to wake up now…Walt! Wake up please! Waaaaalt!" No response and no movement, so I would resort to nudging him, then poking, pushing and tapping him. But to no avail. When he finally resurrected, he would laugh at himself and say he really must work less and sleep more. *Ya think, Walt?*

It wasn't just Mac and Walt who loved to sleep; I would say most people do doze off during their massage even if it's just for a few minutes. But then at the opposite end of that spectrum are those clients who wouldn't dream of missing a moment because there is just too much to talk about. Chatting seems counterintuitive, because massages are supposed to be relaxing, and in school we are taught to create a soothing atmosphere and not to be that annoying therapist who talks all the way through the session. I learned that the biggest complaints people have about massages is that the therapist won't shut up. So, being cognizant of that, I made a point of saying at the beginning of every massage, "If you like, we can chat a little but then we will be quiet so you can relax and enjoy your quiet time."

I think most people are grateful to hear this and to know I won't be babbling on the whole way through, but there are some clients who babble on themselves for the entire duration of their massage. They use this time as their therapy session and they want to talk about everything from their own aches and pains, to their next-door neighbor's affair.

I am quite happy to be a sounding board, and I am ashamed to say that I am more than just a little bit interested in hearing the latest about their neighbor's antics; but to be fair, I do tend to let the client dictate whether they want to chat or be silent. That said, my chatterboxes inevitably take a deep breath in and begin: "So, how are you this week? How was your weekend? How's that lovely husband of yours? And just wait till I tell you what my neighbor did this week…" Sometimes I felt that I should have been paying my clients and not vice versa—for pure entertainment value!

All questions thus far pale in comparison with this next one, the Rolls Royce of questions. People asked frequently when I was a novice massage therapist, and people still ask the same question even now, some 20 years later: "Do guys ever get a woody?" It's the $64,000 question.

Whenever I tell people what I do for a living, they are dying to ask me if my male clients have ever gotten a woody during their massage and if so, how do I handle it? My immediate retort is that indeed I do *not* handle it! There is to be no handling of any woody of any description—ever.

This public curiosity is quite fascinating to be sure, and for some reason it seems to be the first question on everyone's lips—people are dying to know! So, to dispel the myth and satisfy everyone's curiosity, I will give the short answer. In all of my 20 years of being a massage therapist, I can count the number of erections on one hand. Statistically, I'd say that's pretty low. And I shall now tell you the answer to that $64,000 question: What *do* you do when a guy lying naked on your massage table gets a woody?

CHAPTER 7

The penis monologues

"God gave man a penis and a brain, but unfortunately not enough blood supply to run both at the same time."

—Robin Williams

THE PENIS GETS a chapter all its own because unfortunately, and through no fault or solicitation of my own, there have been one or two incidents that I feel are worth mentioning. OK, maybe four. Yes, if I'm perfectly honest, I have four penis sagas to share. As a professional massage therapist, I wish I didn't have any such stories to share, but we don't live in a perfect world. And, seeing as the owners of these male members went to so much trouble to expose themselves, I feel it's only fair to give them some exposure in return.

In addition to being a massage therapist I have also been an instructor at a massage school, so I am justifiably educated regarding the anatomy of the penis. Contrary to popular belief, the penis is technically neither a muscle, nor a bone despite its common nicknames which include "the love muscle" and "boner." As an educator, I feel it's my duty to clear up the misnomer and reveal that the penis is in fact an organ—an external sex organ found only in the male species. It also doubles up as a urine dispenser, so it is essentially quite clever. Perhaps this is why men love to expose it so often? Whatever the reason, it seems to be the most overexposed organ of the human body and is usually presented—solicited or otherwise —with a level of pride and prowess one might expect from a peacock.

The first peacock to expose his pride and joy to me was a client of a high-end gym attached to a hospital in New Jersey. I was new there, and one day during my evening shift in the gym's spa, a male client booked for a post-workout deep tissue massage came sauntering into my room. He began explaining what was ailing him and asked, "Could you go deep into my hamstrings because I just ran an hour on the treadmill? Also, my quads need a good flushing…oh and can you do an abdominal massage too?"

Aghhh, I hated giving men abdominal massages! Nine out of ten of them don't see it as a therapeutic massage designed to aid digestion. No, they see it as a *Close-to-the-Penis Massage.*

I don't mean to sound cynical or judgmental but in my personal experience over the years, this has proven to be the case. I try to give the client the benefit of the doubt when they say they are having digestive issues, but usually I am right and it results in a premeditated woody. And for the massage therapist, a client getting a woody is really, really annoying. And, apart from its close proximity to the toilet parts, a digestive massage couldn't be un-sexier.

For this type of work, we are trained to follow the route of the large intestine and focus on palpating the walls of the ascending colon with the intention of pushing fecal matter around into the transverse colon, and then into the descending colon to promote elimination. Loose translation: we are quite literally moving peoples' shit around! The actual technique is done using three fingertips to push firmly down and knead the abdomen in undulating movements and it can be quite painful depending on the level and duration of the client's constipation.

Trying to put this image out of my mind, I massaged my athlete's hamstrings and quads, stripped the muscles to remove any adhesions in the muscle fibers and flushed them out. Flushing means using fast strokes to push the blood centripetally towards the heart replacing it with fresh oxygened blood. When the new blood whooshes into the muscle tissue, it brings with it fresh nutrients and oxygen which revitalizes and heals. It's genius really and who would have thought that a good rub down could do all this? That's why I love massage; it's magic! I did a good bit of magic on his legs and I felt they would be suppler and pain-free during his next run—mission accomplished! And then, on to the dreaded digestive massage.

As usual when doing digestive massage on my male clients I made sure it was deep and painful and the furthest thing from a sensual massage imaginable, and this gentleman was no exception. I even did the *tapotement*, a loud chopping move, at the end and said, "Well that should sort your digestion out and keep things moving"—a nice reference to bowel movements always adds to the therapeutic intention of it all just so we are on the same page.

"So, you're all done, sir," I said. "I hope you feel better. Thank you and please exit through the men's door. Have a good night."

Done. Over. Phew! *Well that went just fine*, I thought to myself. *No need for me to have been worried or defensive. Or to have dug my fingers so deeply into his intestines. Maybe that was a tad mean and I should try being a little less judgmental and cynical and be a little nicer in future.* These were my thoughts as I washed my hands and then took clean sheets from the drawer for my next client.

It had been ten minutes since I finished my last massage and my next client's session was scheduled to start at the top of the hour. I knocked on the massage room door. No answer. Then I knocked again. I figured my belly massage-loving athlete must be long gone, so with clean sheets under my arms I opened the door and entered. *Dear Lord, but what was this I saw laying before me?*

There was my client lying in wait like a hungry African tiger, ready to startle his next prey. Yes, the animal was on top of the blanket, naked, legs sprawled wide open, playing with his appendage! He had a ridiculous smirk on his face and it was clear that exhibitionism was his M.O. and this obviously wasn't his first time to the rodeo. I guessed he wanted to shock me and get some sort of girly squealing reaction. Instead, all he got was my poker face, my eyebrows unfazed by this pathetic state of affairs, and a business-as-usual retort: "Sir, please do as you are told and exit through the men's locker room door; I have my next client waiting. Thank you."

And with that, I did an about-turn and closed the door. I dashed to the front desk, not because I was shaken or scared, but to see who this clown was. He was obviously a member of the gym so I looked him up on our database. And there he was listed with his wife and two kids as lifelong members: Mr. Ira Goldstein (name changed to protect the guilty). I noticed that he didn't live too far from the gym, and mentally stored the address. Oh, how I would love to go and have a little chat with Mrs. Goldstein, tell her all about her poor husband's digestive problems—maybe even recommend some dietary changes.

I compiled an official complaint and sent it right up to the corporate office. But to no avail. In their infinite wisdom, this was Corporate's response. "We cannot ban him from getting massages because he is a valued lifetime member and we wouldn't want to offend him. Blah, blah, blah…" I stopped reading after that.

Never mind offending *him*, what about the fact that he had offended *me* and demeaned my profession? His exhibitionist behavior constituted sexual harassment. *Moronic corporate imbeciles!* I do hope they don't ever need a massage from me because my elbow might just slip, and I may accidentally knock them off my table or trip with hot stones in my hands and singe their legs.

Upper management never did book a massage in the spa, but I did see our valued customer in the gym one day with his wife and I greeted him accordingly.

"Good evening Mr. Ira Goldstein, and how are we today? Haven't seen you in the spa lately. Hope your *little* problem went away." His wife looked at me confused and then at him. I would have loved to hear what she said to him next, but I darted off rather fast. Amazingly he didn't report me and get me fired and I continued to work at the high-end gym another year. Every time he saw me he pretended he didn't see me, and walked in the opposite direction.

That clown, as ridiculous as his antics were, was amusing if not rather pathetic, and didn't anger me. But another of his fellow species did. This incident happened in Germany when I was still new to the business and worked from home.

On that particular occasion, I thought I had vetted my new client well over the phone; we discussed his sciatica—the main reason for his booking the massage—and I found out where he worked, too. I had taken my usual security measures, leaving the TV on extra loud and parking my car right outside the house so it looked like someone else was home.

In the massage room, we spoke more about the location of his back pain and then I told him I would leave so he could disrobe. I would be back in a few minutes. Just then he whipped out a wad of cash and immediately paid me up front, in full. Right up front like I was a hooker! No one had ever paid up front before because it's not the way we operate in the professional massage industry. That gesture set off a red flag for me and I was on my guard for the first part of the session, but then I thought perhaps I was just being paranoid and proceeded with the massage as normal. Fortunately, it was uneventful, and he slept the whole way through without talking.

Afterwards I said my usual, "I will leave you to get dressed and bring you some water in a few minutes." I gave him ample time to change and then knocked on the door with his glass of water.

He said, "I'm not ready yet." I waited another few minutes and then knocked again. "Just a minute," he said somewhat irritated. How on earth was it taking this guy so long to change? He was only wearing a t-shirt and jeans; it wasn't like he had to put his tie back on. After the third knock, I'd had enough.

Knowing that my next client would be arriving any time, I had to hurry up this guy who seemed to have forgotten how to put on his pants. Without knocking a third time, I simply opened the door and walked in to find him standing with his back turned to me, zipping up his fly rather quickly. He didn't drink his water and with keys in hand, he hurriedly walked past me scuttling down the stairs in awkward silence.

Although I found his behavior odd, I was thankful that his massage was without incident. That was until I returned to the room and found that I was grossly mistaken. And I mean grossly! There had indeed been an incident. Little puddles of semen soiled my sheets. Crumpled up wet tissues lay hidden under the blanket. He had jerked off all over my brand-new Martha Stewart bed linens!

That infuriated me and I was seething; I felt cheap and dirty. I know the work that I do and I know that it is not sleazy, but he made it feel that way and I had to take a shower after he left. I scrubbed my hands until they were red.

This vandal had desecrated my sacred and peaceful massage room, and degraded and debased my business in the process. That was the first time I had felt so affronted in my profession.

Was this the worst job in the world? In what other so-called respectable profession did people have to clean up someone else's sperm? Gross! Disgusting!

My anger subsided over the next few days, but the incident did put me on guard for quite a while afterwards. Lucky for him, Puddles of Semen never called again. I did however, have the rotten misfortune of running into him at the American supermarket on base one Sunday afternoon. The moment I saw his zitty-red face and bulbous nose, I remembered him. He must have felt me glaring at him, seething with squinted eyes, because he looked down and ran to the men's bathroom.

What he hadn't anticipated was me following him in. I pushed the door wide open and blurted out, "How *dare* you be such a pig when you come to get massages! You came to *my house* and insulted me and degraded my industry!"

He looked up, down and around for another way to escape from the men's toilets and from my wrath. His face turned the hue of a freshly-slapped bottom and he covered his eyes with his hand. Speaking down to the floor, he mumbled "I don't know what you are talking about."

The other men in mid-urination at their urinals looked at me, then at him, then back at me wondering what was going on as I continued hurling abuse.

"You disrespectful, lame excuse for a man!"

"Whoa…what did this guy do?" one urinating patron asked.

"He came to my practice for a professional massage and the bastard ejaculated all over my sheets. Yes, you heard me correctly," I said.

The lame excuse ran out of the men's room. In embarrassing him, I felt vindicated. Admittedly, I may have embarrassed myself a little in the process yelling in public, but at least I had exposed him for the pig that he was. As I looked around me at my audience, I noticed they were all well dressed and conservative-looking as if they had just come from church. I realized that it was indeed Sunday and this was indeed the church crowd buying their weekly groceries after Mass. Oh dear.

Regaining my composure, I thought it best to leave quickly and quietly. I convinced myself that God would forgive me for my public outburst, and that surely, He would have wanted me to teach this wayward member of the flock a lesson.

I am sad to say that this was not the only saga in which my sheets and my pride got soiled. A similar occurrence happened about five years later in New Jersey soon after another military move.

The genius's name was Nico. He was from Greece, jolly and overweight with a goatee and reminded me of Santa Claus. During his massage, Nico and I chatted about how much both my father and I loved his country and that Dad spoke Greek so well that he prided himself on being able to order boiled potatoes in restaurants rather than the usual British tourist staple of chips, chips, and more chips. The jolly Greek was impressed by my knowledge and love of Greek food and we talked at length about how to make the perfect Moussaka. Towards the end of the massage he asked if I would massage his stomach to help with his digestion. Nico said he had read about how effective digestive massage was in keeping oneself healthy. As he seemed so knowledgeable about the benefits, I assumed he received regular stomach massages and thought nothing of it.

Using two towels, one laying across his chest and the other above his pelvic girdle, I moved to the stomach and began the digestive massage protocol tracing the direction of the large intestine to help stimulate the muscle contractions of the colon. It's funny that I can actually feel the pulse of the tissue and any obstructions. I am sure the clients on the receiving end of the stomach massage are unaware that I can actually feel the location of their problematic hardened fecal matter and I wonder what they would think if they knew. *I'm just moving your shit around. You're welcome!*

I don't know what Nico was thinking because for this part he was silent with his eyes closed, presumably sleeping. The massage came to an end and my new Greek friend paid me and gave me a hefty $50 tip. He said he felt great and that he intended to incorporate massages into his weekly schedule because that was the best massage he had ever had. I was flattered. I bid him farewell and returned to my room to get ready for my afternoon sessions, and then head out for some lunch. I grabbed the rolled-up sheets to dump them in the laundry basket quickly before leaving and realized to my horror that they felt strange—too cold and way too... wet. I immediately threw them on the floor and unrolled them to find what could only be a small pool of sperm.

The fat fuck has ejaculated all over my sheets!

God, I hated my job right now—this *was* the worst profession in the world! I held back angry tears as I threw the sheets in the dumpster outside and stewed all afternoon over what a bad judge of character I was and how naïve I was and how—again—some stupid guy had duped me into giving him a *Close to the Penis Massage* under the guise of digestive therapy. That was it: from here on out, I would never perform digestive massages on any more male clients—no matter how constipated they were.

I was so mad that I couldn't let the incident go. I called Nico later that evening. Mounted high on my horse, I lashed out at him, saying how dare he disrespect me, and how dare he insult an educated professional! I went on and on about how disgusted and offended I felt without letting him get a word in, and was about to slam the phone down when he sheepishly apologized and begged my forgiveness. He said he couldn't help it, that his ejaculation was an involuntary reaction because touching the stomach was so stimulating. He was embarrassed and seemed very remorseful, vowing it would never happen again and pleaded with me to give him one more chance. Now, I certainly do acknowledge that getting an erection can be a normal physiological response and yes, sometimes involuntary. Also, I am not a prude and am more liberal than most. Besides, I like to think that I am a very forgiving person and so, against my better judgment, I gave him the benefit of the doubt.

A few months later Nico came back and neither of us mentioned his prior physiological response. Since our last interlude I had moved offices and was now sharing space with a chiropractor.

Since his back was in bad shape, Nico had decided to get a massage followed by a chiropractic adjustment with Doctor Bill downstairs. As usual he was chatty and very pleasant and said that in all the years of getting massages, no one massaged as well as I did. That was a very nice compliment and I appreciated it. After his session, he got dressed, paid me and handed me another big tip and I escorted him to the waiting room. Back up in my room I grabbed the sheets which were crumpled up and rolled into a big ball, and wet...*No, he couldn't possibly...he wouldn't...he DID!* The little SHIT!

I stood there, blood boiling, not knowing quite how to handle the situation. But I was too mad to let it go this time and my vengeful, mean streak raised its ugly head. Stuffing the soaked sheets into a plastic bag, I waltzed back downstairs into the crowded waiting room and said loudly for all to hear, "I believe these sperm-filled wet sheets are yours. YOU wash them and keep them, and don't ever come back! Go and find yourself another massage therapist!"

I shoved the bag in his face—wet side up—stormed out, and that was that. Strangely enough, after being humiliated before a waiting room audience of chiropractic patients, Jolly Jism-the-Greek never bothered me again. And I somehow went right off my Moussaka.

About a year later in the same office, a two-story converted Victorian house in an affluent neighborhood, I took a last-minute booking from someone who had found my name through a Google search. I wasn't paying for these search results, but if it was a Google oversight, I wasn't complaining because it brought me a constant stream of new clients. I booked the massage for exactly 6:50 p.m., which is an odd time, but I knew at this hour, the two doctors and their receptionists would still be on the premises. Plus, there would still be a few clients in the waiting area. My new client would see that the office was full of people, and was a legitimate, bustling medical practice. I hoped this would deter him from pulling any funny stuff. This was my sense of security.

The problem was that an hour later after the massage was over, everyone—and I mean *everyone*, including the cleaners—had gone home and I was all alone in the building with a total stranger. This was the part of having my own massage practice that I hated. As a preemptive measure, I always left specific instructions for the chiropractors to leave the lights and the radio on when they went home; they knew the drill. On this particular evening, I was upstairs in my own massage office with this new client—an Indian businessman from Philly—and all was going well until about half-way through the massage. For whatever reason, he thought it would be a good strategy to start fondling his penis under the sheets. I thought that was a very *bad* strategy and I was in no mood to tolerate such antics, so I immediately removed his offending right arm and placed it firmly on top of the blanket. A few minutes later he tried the same stunt with his left arm. I put that arm on top of the blanket too. Once again, he slipped his right arm under the sheet for the trifecta. I couldn't help but be reminded of the Hindu deity with the six arms. What was his name, Ganesh? I said sternly, "Time to turn over now." He grunted and tutted under his breath, obviously frustrated that I was disturbing his little game, but he complied nonetheless.

With him facing down I could place his hands above his head, resting on the armrest and nowhere near any low-hanging genitalia. At this point I really wanted to put a strategically placed elbow sharply into his spine or press my thumb into his jugular vein at the front of his neck with extreme force. In a perfect world, I would have done just that, but in this world where people sue because their coffee is too hot and no one told them they might get burned, I didn't want to risk any legal ramifications for asphyxiating my client. I stopped fantasizing about doing him in and instead, gave him a rushed, crappy massage, cutting the session short. Afterwards, in a very business-like fashion, I told him to get dressed and meet me down at reception when he was ready. He handed me his credit card and I exited the room.

Instinct told me that I should take extra precautions because I couldn't read this guy sent by Google, and so I ran down the stairs, unlocked the back door and left it wide open with my car running at the back of the building in the unlit parking lot. Being extra vigilant, I also left open the front door which faced the main busy street.

At reception, I quickly ran his credit card through the machine and as I did, a thought came into my head, and I must say it was a stroke of genius on my part. He hadn't asked over the phone how much the session was going to be, so he didn't know that it was only $75—for all he knew it could have been $150. Yes, $150 seemed like a perfectly fair number after his disruptive and disorderly behavior.

He paid, said nothing and walked out the door. I immediately locked it, watched him drive off and then sprinted out the back door. Diving into my car, I sped off, thanking God and Ganesh for my safe escape.

My penis stories have given me much fodder for ridicule over the last twenty years, and I have lived to tell the tales. I know I am fortunate to have come through unscathed, and as funny as the tales may be after the fact, they were unnerving at the time. Being an experienced therapist and therefore older and wiser, has made me better equipped to handle such situations—not that I ever did *handle* any of these situations, just for the record.

Sadly, young female massage therapists new to the career field have been damaged by incidents like mine. For inexperienced graduates, one bad experience can put an end to their careers before they have even had a fair chance to prosper. All that schooling and all that money gone to waste—not to mention their professional dream shattered because a client decided to behave inappropriately or even worse, in a threatening manner. It's understandable that this would leave a bitter taste in the beginner therapists' mouths that just won't subside. But more than that, their passion withers and dies.

People like the constipated athlete, Puddles of Semen, Jolly Jism-the-Greek and Ganesh, the Indian businessman, thought they were just being brazen and cocky, probably seeing how much they could get away with. They obviously had some serious issues with deviant behavior. But, it also begs the question: why even involve the massage table?

You don't even need a massage table to entertain yourself in that way. Go to clubs displaying luminescent pink lights outside with names like Chubby's, Fatty's, or Volcanic Eruptions and erupt there!

I'm not criticizing the gentlemen who like to frequent these establishments—Baskin Robbins has 31 flavors to appeal to all tastes, and I suppose massage is no different. But I do criticize those gentlemen who come to legitimate massage therapists and push their luck. I've only had to deal with a few deviants over the span of my career, which works out to about one penis story every four years. And I have to admit; these stories do make great party conversation. That said, these offending male members need to be put in their place—safely tucked away in a pair of underpants—and not poking out of the top of my sheets on the massage table.

Before I put the subject of the penis down—so to speak — one last important thing to understand is that the people who perpetrated those acts are not representative of my clientele over the years. And despite how annoying and even disturbing their behavior may have been, they neither tainted nor tarnished my love of my trade. I refused to let them shame me or make me feel insecure; their perception of my work is irrelevant. I can proudly say I have conquered the love muscle, the boner, the organ—whatever you want to call it, and it was no match for me. Peacocks of this world, you are on notice: do not mess with the massage therapist—you will not win and your delicate plumage will be squashed. Literally.

CHAPTER 8

Will work for meatballs

"Massage therapy was a $12.1 billion industry in 2015."
—American Massage Therapy Association (AMTA)

PUTTING ASIDE ALL the maddening massage misconceptions and fallacies borne out of ignorance from a small, misguided population, I chose to ignore my own inner insecurities about what others thought and focus on the joys of my trade instead. I have always been proud to bring the gift of relaxation, stress relief and pain management to my clients, and when they left my massage room, I felt like I had made a difference. And the added bonus? The money was good, too. Mostly...

I never went into the field thinking that rubbing people could possibly be lucrative; I just did it at first because I loved the human touch and it wasn't a boring office job. I figured I'd make enough money to buy a round of beers down the pub, but I never dreamed of pulling in $2000 in one day. Or getting paid in the currency of meatballs for that matter!

People often wonder how much money massage therapists actually make and often times the answer shocks them. It's a difficult question to answer because all massage therapists are not created equal: an experienced therapist with her own practice will inevitably make more than someone working in a salon or spa working for someone else. And therapists specializing in pregnancy massage or sports massage, for example, might make a lot more than their peers. And, strangely enough, our pay tends to go up and down according to the season. Or even with the change of weather.

For my part, some days I make enough for a long weekend for two in the Bahamas, but other days I make just enough for a large pepperoni and mushroom pizza. Early on in my career, I realized that the massage business could be a bit of a financial roller coaster ride, and if I was going to make it a full-time job that paid the bills, I was going to have to think like a business owner. Sales and marketing would be crucial.

In the early days in my practice in Germany, I did what most massage therapists do—I offered products for sale in my office. It's quite common to sell anything from Bengay-type sports creams, massage oils, and essential oils, to diet products, cosmetics, handbags and accessories. As I did facials using the Dermalogica skin care line, I sold the whole line of products, too: cleansers, moisturizers, masks, zit concealers and anti-aging creams. When my clients saw how vibrant and clear their skin looked after their treatments, it was fairly easy to sell the products. Retail was the way to go.

I also sold homemade heat packs for the neck which my craft-loving 70-year-old friend, Pauline, had made for me. These were microwaveable beanbags made of wheat kernels scented with lavender, and each bag came in a different color and pattern. At only $20 each, they didn't sit long enough to gather dust on my shelves.

Then I got a little more creative. I introduced Pashmina shawls for a while (of all things) and they were my biggest moneymaker yet. I know selling shawls in a massage office may seem slightly odd, but they were the height of fashion in the States at the time.

Besides, my friend's mum was an expat there and she would ship me the real deal at Indian prices. One corner of my massage room burst with bright, colorful soft cashmere shawls and they sold fast, especially at Christmas.

Christmas in Germany was hugely successful for my business. One day during the festive season, Santa came early, and brought me the busiest, most profitable day since first opening.

On a freezing cold mid-December evening after a full twelve-hour day of working until nine o'clock at night, I sat down and calculated my earnings for the day. In addition to rubbing eight bodies, I had also sold skincare sets, massage oils, beanbags and shawls—all gift-wrapped with big red bows. I had made $2,000 in total; I could hardly believe it!

Christmas has always been my busiest time of year and in order to be prepared for the influx of the season's business, I had to start getting ready in October.

My first order of business was getting my bottles in. No, not my bottles of festive booze like Bailey's, Brandy, Gluhwein and the like, nor bottles of massage oil—just plain, empty bottles. Empty bottles are not a typical order for massage therapists, but for the last twelve years I have been selling my Christmas gift certificates in bottles. I call them Massage-in-a-Bottle and it's been a genius marketing strategy.

I didn't come up with this genius strategy; that was my friend Don who I used to work with, and it has been a wonderful money-spinning approach for the holidays. The certificates look like any other in that they have a "to" and "from" and a space for the type of massage purchased, but the certificate is rolled up, tied with a ribbon and bottled to make it look like a message in a bottle brought in by the tide. Then the bottle is corked and labeled with my business logo to look like a wine label. I even put little shells in the bottle to make it beachy, like it just washed up on the shore. People think it's a message in a bottle, but it's not a *message*, it's a *massage.* At the spa. Clients go mad over this novel idea and the bottles sell like hotcakes almost immediately.

For a time, when we were living in New Jersey and stationed at McGuire Air Force base, the name of my business was *The English Touch* and the boxes of bottles would arrive, addressed to the *English Touch Distillery.* Maybe they thought I was making English-style festive booze? During the lead-up to the holidays, I would sit at my kitchen table at night sticking labels onto my bottles and tying ribbons onto my dollar store gift bags. Then I'd arrange all the bags and bottles on the shelves in my office with a big sign, "Massage Gift Certificates on Sale Now!" There would be so many crowding the shelves and stocked in drawers, but by December 23rd, if not earlier, the last one would fly off the shelf. I even offered free delivery to local homes or businesses if people bought two or more; I was Santa delivering sacks of relaxation to my clients!

One year two days before Christmas, a car salesman called and asked if he could stop by to pick up a gift certificate for his wife. He was a new client and had found me online. I was one of the closest places to his office and he said he had left his shopping to the last minute, as usual. I was just finishing up before closing for Christmas because I don't like to work Christmas Eve, so he only just caught me.

The young car salesman in his gray full-length wool coat bought two bottles, one for his wife and one for his girlfriend (no judgment!) Then, he asked, "Do you have any more? Because I have a showroom full of guys at the dealership who haven't had time to go out shopping for their wives either."

"I have some more bottles at home", I lied. "I could meet you in your office in thirty minutes?"

I had no more bottles left to sell but I did have a plan. I rushed home and fished ten empty wine bottles out of the trash from a party we had thrown the weekend before, hoping that ten would be enough. I wiped them down and stuck my labels on the front and with one quick stop at the dollar store for cheap glitzy gift bags, I was ready to go.

At the dealership, it was like Christmas Eve at the mall with overworked car salesmen frantically buying up massages and facials for their wives and mothers. It took less than half an hour to sell the last of my bottles and, quite unexpectedly, I made an extra $1000 that day. Everyone thanked me for being their savior, happy they were spared fighting the last-minute crowds.

It's not just the moneymaking opportunities that I love about the festive season; I love how the work can be so varied and random. And when I say random, I mean that I once got paid in meatballs—kind of.

It was in New Jersey during the holidays and I got a call from the owner of one of the busiest Italian restaurants in town. He asked if I could come to the restaurant for a day and pamper his staff as part of an employee appreciation day and special holiday gift.

This should be fun, I thought to myself. I told him it would be $75 an hour and I would waive the travel fee. He agreed and we scheduled for the following week. When the day came, I set up in the banquet room in the back of the restaurant where I lit candles, put on music and made it cozy. I began at nine in the morning, and by six in the evening, I had indulged the waiters and waitresses, the managers, the cashiers, the custodians and the chefs. I had massaged back-to-back all day long with no time for lunch and barely a bathroom break. Everyone was relaxed. I was ravenous.

It had been a novelty to work in a restaurant for the day and it was a welcome change of scenery from my office. But the downside was that all day I had been cruelly tortured by the smell of all that scrumptious food coming from the kitchen and I would have killed for a bowl of spaghetti or some shrimp scampi. Instead of killing anyone, I decided to round up some friends and come back to the restaurant for dinner because the food looked so good—especially the home-made meatballs the size of footballs. Before I left, the manager paid me my $675 fee and tipped me $200. On top of that he gave me $200 worth of gift certificates which I planned to spend on their famous meatballs that evening. I was so excited to get back and eat! I rushed home, took a shower and rushed right back there with my husband and friends in tow.

It was my treat and I had every intention of using up all of my certificates that night. The food was served family style and we ordered the works: chicken parmesan, seafood linguine, caprese salad, lasagna and of course the meaty footballs. And to wash that down we spared no expense ordering copious amounts of wine.

The owner, a portly and cheerful Italian man who looked like he hadn't missed a meal greeted us and did something I never expected: he comped our entire dinner, grateful I had taken care of his staff. I had been paid, and then paid again in meatballs and pasta. That day I had made over $1000 when all was said and done, and four of us got tipsy on wine and stuffed to the gills for free. It was days like these when I thought I had the best job in the world!

The lucrative day at the Italian restaurant was indeed a feast in more ways than one. But I know that just as business can be a feast, it can just as easily be a famine. Especially in January, when everyone is spent out and broke, up to their eyeballs in debt from the holidays and as such, the massage world is quiet. And it's a famine during snowstorms, too: January and snowstorms suck!

I remember most of my famines took place in Germany. One winter day I looked at my schedule and saw that I had a full day booked, and I was ready for a long day of massaging six clients. Then I looked out the window and saw that it had started snowing, but only lightly—nothing to be alarmed about. Until the phone rang. And then, not only was it snowing but it was raining too. Raining on my parade.

That's when the first call came in from one of my regulars. "Hi, it's Susan. I am going to have to cancel my appointment this morning because the roads look too dangerous."

The snow wasn't even settling but what could I say? What I wanted to say was, *"If you were in Nebraska you'd know what heavy snowfall was and you'd have to put chains on your tires just to leave the house."* But instead, I said, "No problem. Stay warm and I will see you next week."

As the morning went on, the snow fell harder and thicker and my phone rang again. And again. First it was Doyle who had a Porsche and he didn't want to risk driving when the roads were slippery. I couldn't blame him for that. Then Jan, my three o'clock cancelled because she heard that the weatherman had forecasted eight inches of snow by the afternoon and she didn't want to drive in her new Volvo.

Why did I have to have clients with such posh cars? Now I was down three massages but still had three remaining clients all due to come in later that afternoon and evening. However, as the snow fell, the phone rang and by lunchtime, scared off by the pesky, fear-mongering weatherman, all six of my clients had rescheduled.

The snowstorm had dumped itself on my doorstep and stayed there rent-free for the best part of a week. Living in Albersbach, one of the tiniest villages in the Rheinland Pfalz, we were always one of the last to have our streets plowed, so the roads became ice rinks, and no one was getting in or out very easily during a snowstorm— least of all my clients. Everyone stayed home, presumably keeping warm with their log fires a-blazing. Schools closed and the base operated with essential personnel only.

No one was thinking about massages except for me, which meant I was making zero dollars multiplied by seven days. Professionally speaking, I was in starvation mode and if the storm didn't pass soon, I'd be eating instant noodles out of polystyrene cups, and everyone knows that's far worse than a famine!

I just hated that irksome feeling that I was a failure when I had slow weeks generating no money at all; what skilled, smart therapist made a zero-dollar salary? In times like these, I felt even more inadequate knowing that some of my high school friends back in England made more in end-of-year bonuses in their big corporate positions than I made in an entire year. That could have been me. Should it have been me? There was that thought again tugging at my conscience–that I wasn't reaching my true potential and that massaging would never be enough. But, it wasn't as if I would be doing this forever; the novelty would undoubtedly soon wear off and I'd get a steady job with a steady income and I wouldn't have to worry about snowstorms. But for now, I had to remind myself that sometimes I had to suck it up, stop sulking and take the good with the bad. I have no problem taking the good with the bad…it's the sulking part I'm still working on.

Looking on the bright side, I also had to remind myself that whether I was broke, rolling in cash, or working for meatballs, I truly loved the variety of my work. One thing is for sure: the world of massage is never boring. Each day, each season, each client and each treatment are unique. And who knows what shenanigans the next day might bring, or who I might meet?

CHAPTER 9

Around the world on a massage table

"Life is either a daring adventure or nothing."

—Helen Keller

As MUCH AS I like to give massages, I love to be on the receiving end too, and I make a point of getting a massage almost everywhere I go. I see it as research. I love to check out what my counterparts are doing, and maybe steal some of their moves while I am at it.

I find that the best time for me to get a massage is when I'm on vacation, when I know no one is going to disturb me, and because I travel frequently, I have treated myself to many different kinds of massages all over the world. I have been pampered, rubbed, touched, felt-up, squeezed and beaten in various types of establishments and settings in different countries, and not all of them were pleasant experiences. I have received an indulgent massage at a five-star Caribbean resort; a cheap head massage and neck-cracking at a Muay Thai boxing match in Thailand; naked massages, ice plunges; and unfortunately, I have had endured having my nipples tweaked quite by mistake in Egypt.

Even though all these treatments fall under the same umbrella, and fit the definition of massage, no two were alike and it's hard to say which one I liked the most. It is impossible to compare the different types of bodywork. Trying to compare massages is like trying to compare cake.

Think of cake for a moment. It can conjure up an exhibition hall of images in your mind because you could be talking about vanilla sponge cake, tiramisu, fresh cream meringue, or at the very bottom of the cake hierarchy, a Twinkie. But you'd still be talking about cake. And just like cake, massage also encompasses a variety of choices: from oil to clothed; from aromatherapy to hydrotherapy; from dimly lit spas to clinical medical offices; from soothing strokes to chopping moves, and it would be wrong to compare them or judge them by the same yardstick.

A Hawaiian Lomi Lomi massage with its smooth, flowing strokes is completely different from a myofascial release massage, which is more medically focused. In the same vein, one cannot compare a sensual, relaxing aromatherapy with lavender to stretching the legs over the head in a remedial sports massage. It is hard to compare a homemade dessert made with love to a highly processed mass-produced snack with a shelf life of twenty-five years. It's a matter of taste and mood, so when people say they just don't like massages in general, it's an uneducated statement. Just like when people say they don't like cake, it just cannot possibly be…

Depending upon where I am and on my mood, sometimes I will order the Black Forest gateau of treatments and sometimes I will simply opt for the frozen cheesecake; both hit the spot, but the experience is entirely different.

The most expensive massage of the Black Forest gateau variety that I ever received was at a five-star spa on Peter Island in the Virgin Islands. It cost me two hundred smackers and unfortunately, it was more like a boxed donut than the rich German chocolate cake I'd craved. The experience started off well and had much potential. The glossy brochure at reception touted the spa as "a tropical sanctuary" and told me to immerse myself in paradise and get lost in my thoughts, promising me a "rejuvenating, sensual journey."

Sold!

Upon entering the spa, there was an air of sophistication; the décor of the dressing room with its candles and floral arrangements was elegant, luxurious and classy—everything you would expect from a spa of such caliber. The elegance continued as I walked out into the cliff-top gardens along the flower-lined pathways surrounded by lush, brightly colored plants leading to a pool with waterfalls cascading down.

It was paradise, heaven on earth, and exactly how I imagined the Garden of Eden. I stopped to relax on the chaise longue and listen to the gentle music playing before I eased into the whirlpool built into the rocks, with sweeping views overlooking the sparkling blue-green Caribbean Sea.

I could have spent all day in those blissful surroundings, but it was almost time for my massage appointment. And if my spa experience was anything to go by, it was going to be a real treat. I had booked the deep tissue massage to get myself ironed out because I was stiff from sleeping on a catamaran for the last week, sailing around the British Virgin Islands with a group of friends. According to the brochure the deep tissue massage sounded like just what I needed: "a firmer massage designed to relieve aching muscles as well as every day stress and promote detoxification— the pathway to a clear body and mind." Oh yes, that would do me just fine.

I walked my aching muscles into the tropical-themed room where floor to ceiling windows revealed a beautiful garden on the other side. I stood in awe at how elegantly the massage table was set up with a flower on the pillow and batik-style covers, and I made a mental note to put a flower on my own pillows for my clients when I got back home. I'd have liked to have had a private little garden outside my office window too, but that was most definitely not in my budget. As I climbed on the table and under the sheets I felt warm from some kind of heating element on the table, adding to my comfort. How could I have expected anything less from a five-star spa?

I explained to the male therapist that my neck and shoulders were tight and needed some deep work and then I stopped talking, figuring his hands would deduce the rest. No need to micromanage; these five-star therapists were trained professionals and must be world class to work in a place like this. After five minutes of warm up effleurage strokes—the long soothing strokes of Swedish massage designed to introduce the hands to the body and begin a treatment—I was ready for some actual remedial therapy to relieve me of my poor stiff neck and knotted shoulders. But to my frustration, the light soothing strokes continued. The clock was ticking and about $50 into my massage—precisely fifteen minutes at their price—I piped up with, "Umm, I need the massage to be much deeper, please, especially on my shoulders. Could you just focus on the knots in my shoulders?"

He said yes, but his hands said no: mind and body were clearly not on the same page. Finally, at about the $75 mark, the massage got deeper, but not in a good way. Using both elbows, my five-star therapist dug into my trapezius sliding down my back between the shoulder blades and then dragged the elbows back up using full force. One cannot physically go any further down the back with this move without losing leverage and collapsing in a big heap on top of the client—not exactly standard procedure. It's a really awful move if done incorrectly and this was being done incorrectly.

I'd had enough. My inner brat just couldn't help herself, and she blurted out, "You can't keep doing the same move over and over. It's painful and this is definitely *not* a deep tissue massage."

The tall, skinny man, in a local Caribbean accent apologized, but it was too late; he and his bony-elbows had succeeded in annoying and un-relaxing me at the same time, and I was beyond disappointed. He tried a different stroke, but I could tell he didn't have many more moves up his sleeve. It became apparent that the decadent gateau I was expecting was nothing more than a plain donut, and it didn't even have the jelly inside. I had been duped!

Sulking and with the knots in my shoulders very much intact, I headed towards reception to reluctantly pay for my $200 massage. I couldn't help but notice that the sun still shone brightly in the sky, proof positive this had indeed been daylight robbery! When the receptionist asked me, "And how was your massage today madam?" my inner brat reared her ugly little head once again and said, "Quite horrible actually and not what I'd expect from a world-class resort. The therapist was inexperienced and kept sticking his knobby elbows into my back. It was not what I signed up for."

I saw by her contorted face that she had taken offense and so I felt the need to add, "Well, you did ask."

Clearly customer service was a foreign concept to her because she, in her infinite ignorance, replied haughtily, "All of our guests enjoy our massages and you are the only one that didn't." *Oh, really? The only one?* Somehow, I didn't think so and I could bet on two things at this point: first, she was telling big fat lies and second, she had never had a massage herself from any of the knobbly-elbowed therapists. If she had, Ms. sour-faced receptionist would have known that unlike what the brochure promised, that massage was, in fact, a detour from the "pathway to a clear body and mind." And how dare she be so rude? Well, I could stoop to her level. Seeing her rudeness and raising her sarcasm, I retaliated.

"Listen, dear…I am an experienced and licensed massage therapist with my own practice and I am national board certified. So, I do know what I am talking about. You, on the other hand, obviously do not. The massage was God-awful and you just stole $200 from my pocket. And with that attitude, might I suggest that you get a massage yourself?"

With that, I turned on my heel and walked out to head back

to the boat. It was time for some much-needed Caribbean rum, which at $15.99 a bottle was much better value than my massage.

My Virgin Island five-star massage was the most expensive massage I ever had and one of the most disappointing. Ironically, the cheapest massage I ever had was one of the most effective, proving that you don't always get what you pay for.

I wasn't even planning on getting a massage that summer night in Pattaya, Thailand. Food was the first thing on my mind and massage was the last as I ventured out to visit the night markets. My husband and I were staying in a local bed and breakfast for a week-long anniversary getaway. He was sleeping and I was starving. Much like a farmer's market, night markets are an experience in themselves. Locals flaunt their artistic wares and the aromas of roasting street food fill the air. I was wandering around aimlessly, sampling all the food I could and drinking Thailand's own Tsing Tao beer.

With a full belly, I made my way over to the busiest part of the night market where Thai boxing was about to take place. It was Muay Thai and the boxers were young Thai boys: one in red silky shorts and one in blue. They fought round after round, cheered on ceremoniously by the crowd. The whole scene was very colorful, animated, and loud. The Thais are fanatical about their national sport.

As I sat ringside on one of the round, red metal stools watching the fight, I was approached by one of the local ladies who was making her rounds giving seated massages. She came armed with oil, towels and a pink plastic bucket full of hot water. Massages cost a mere $5. My shoulders needed some TLC, so I said yes.

As I sat watching the boys kick each other in the shins, throwing punches to each other's face and upper cuts to each other's jaw, I received a glorious head massage. The petite lady with delicate hands wrapped hot towels around my face. Ahh, it was bliss. I tuned out, soon becoming oblivious to my surroundings. That was until I heard the crowd roar and clap and I opened my eyes just in time to see a brutal kick with the knee to the side of the face from Red Shorts, and retaliation straight back from Blue Shorts: a roundhouse high kick slapping the back of his opponent's head causing him to drop to the ground instantly, making a rather loud thud. The crowd cheered once more.

Ouch, that had to hurt. Bet he is seeing stars right about now… glad it wasn't my head.

My own head, by comparison, felt very light and relaxed. The Thai lady pressed points on my brows and cheekbones and then proceeded to rub my temples quite vigorously. Now I was the one seeing stars! Surely that wasn't normal and I hoped she wasn't going to charge me extra. Luckily, she stopped and then proceeded to take out her little pot of Tiger Balm to massage my neck and shoulders.

The concoction smelled like an antiseptic ointment with a minty freshness to it and felt tingly on my skin. Tiger Balm is touted in Thailand as a cure-all and the locals rub it anywhere for any ailment: nausea, constipation, (diarrhea too) and it even doubles up as a paint thinner.

As I inhaled the paint-thinning balm and mused over all its magical medicinal properties, my masseuse grabbed my head and folded it into her crossed arms.

Oh…umm…OK, that's different…

Then to my surprise, but more to my alarm, she swung around and I heard a series of loud cracks: the pint-sized lady had just given me a chiropractic adjustment! Well, I was not expecting that at all; in fact, it had come as a bit of a shock. She finished off with some chopping on my upper back just to make sure my muscles were truly tenderized like a well-pounded schnitzel, and she must have either been very satisfied with her work or amused at my dazed expression because she giggled to herself as she picked up her bucket.

As if the Muay Thai boxing wasn't entertaining enough, I'd had a spa party of my very own going on in my seat. It was well worth the $5 and the fighting was free. It went down as the cheapest and most entertaining night out I'd had in a long time.

As a licensed massage therapist, I can tell a good massage from a bad one and who is and isn't experienced. With the Thai women, I am pretty sure they were not licensed, nor did they have formal training. I'd bet too they couldn't name the muscles they were massaging.

Instead, I would guess the trade had been passed down from generation to generation, because as unconventional as it was, they knew what they were doing. The result of this empirical training was that stiff shoulders were made soft, tight backs were made supple again, and misaligned bones were put back into place. Do I think that the ladies with pink buckets should be doing chiropractic adjustments at the side of boxing rings? Probably not. But would I recommend the experience? Absolutely!

Receiving massages in different countries is one of my favorite things to do; it's such a cultural delight!

In the land of the Pharaohs, I was fortunate enough to enjoy two culturally delightful massage experiences, and they were very different from each other. The first one was given by a woman at the Meridian Hotel in Cairo, at the foot of the pyramids, and the second one was in a hotel in Sharm El Sheik, down south in the Sinai desert, given by a man.

At the hotel in Cairo I went down to the spa to book my very first Egyptian massage. I asked what kinds of massage they offered.

"Natural massage," the receptionist stated nonchalantly.

"Oh, right. Do you have any other types?"

"Only natural massage. Woman massage woman."

I had no choice but to go with the natural massage and assumed that it was the culture that dictated that women massage women, while men massage men, and I had no preference, so it was fine with me. My massage was at two o'clock which meant I had time to lounge by the pool for part of the afternoon. What a gorgeous pool that was with its swim-up bar in the center and the pyramids at Giza looming large as life over the blue water! I felt like I was right at the foot of the monument itself even though I must have been at least a mile away. I marveled like one is supposed to do at the pyramids, one of the seven ancient wonders of the world. I marveled until it was time for my massage and I made my way inside.

I waited in the spa and noticed an Egyptian woman entering wearing a jogging suit. A jogging suit in 100-degree heat. *Weird attire for a spa.* She then introduced herself as my massage therapist. *So, this is what a natural massage therapist looks like. It's not what I would wear to work, but never mind. When in Rome...*

We went into a simple room with a massage table—nothing fancy—and I lay down naked with only a small hand towel which barely covered my voluptuous bottom. My therapist wasn't very feminine. Truth be told she was hefty, serious and all business. I was quite sure I was going to get quite a pounding. And I was right.

The massage started a little rough. She used fast, furious strokes, like she was in a hurry. It must have been a workout for her because she was sweating profusely and took her jacket off, continuing to massage matter-of-factly in just her bra and jogging bottoms. It was unconventional and slightly amusing, but I kept my grin to myself because she looked like she could make mincemeat out of me.

Throughout the massage, she didn't let up and rubbed vigorously, wiping the sweat off her brow with a towel at regular intervals. When my 90 minutes were up, she stood drenched and must have been exhausted. I was worn out too after being pounded and flogged and thumped.

Strangely enough I was grateful for the beating because she had clobbered any stress and pain out of me. I felt light, intoxicated. I couldn't even move my mouth to speak when I got back to my hotel room. Flopping on the bed, I passed out like a nurse had given me morphine and I slept until dinner time. My husband had never seen me so serene or docile in our whole marriage, and in his quest for a bit of quiet time, he kindly booked me in for another massage the next day.

My second experience with Egyptian massage was in Sharm El Sheik in the Sinai desert. Unlike that first massage, it was a tad strange and wasn't natural. No, I was having an unnatural massage by a man. A man named Abdul.

I told Abdul that I, too, was a professional massage therapist, but his English fell into the completely crap category to say the least and he just smiled, apparently with no clue what I had just said. So, I pointed to myself and waving my hands, I announced "Me, massage therapist."

After giving my pre-massage briefing I closed my eyes and shut up. The Egyptian massage wasn't as good as the one I'd had in Cairo, but I couldn't criticize the massage itself. The strokes were acceptable, but the masseur pushed the boundary when it came to massaging my chest.

A chest massage means pecs—the pectoralis major and pectoralis minor muscles which happen to be located behind the breast tissue. The idea is for the therapist to sit at the top end of the table and to massage with the knuckles so fingers don't get in the way and the client feels comfortable knowing she isn't going to get groped. But Abdul wasn't following protocol that day. He started with the pecs but then went in between my breasts, essentially massaging my cleavage.

On no page in any massage manual in the U.K. or the U.S. of A. does there say anything about cleavage massage. Maybe it was different in Egypt? But the cleavage massage was followed by a sweeping move from under my armpits to the middle of my chest thereby cupping both breasts and swinging them back and forth like a hammock.

Now I am very liberal and I like to think of myself as culturally sensitive, but even *I* thought this was a bit much. I drew the line when he started tweaking my nipples with his fingers and thumbs! Surely this guy must have been having a laugh at my expense?

Nipple play was way out of his scope of practice so I turned onto my stomach for the remainder of the session, keeping my

breasts squashed and out of reach. It wasn't that he was a bad massage therapist per se, but I do think he was trying to pull a fast one
with tourists under the guise of the massage being "Egyptian" and
probably different from what they were used to. As I was leaving the
spa I noticed that Abdul's next client was an American man and I
wondered if he was going to get his nipples tweaked, too. I thought
about warning the unsuspecting tourist but decided it was none of
my business and went on my merry way to the café next door, going
from one cultural experience to another: eating Egyptian hummus,
pita bread, and some shawarma on a stick.

Egypt wasn't the only time I have had my breasts fully fondled
during a massage. The other was during a visit to Paris to see my sis-
ter, Kate, who lived there. One of the top tourist recommendations
was to visit the Turkish Hammam in the famous Blue Mosque and
get a massage. A massage in Paris! *Que magnifique!*

Before any of the massage or spa treatments, we embraced the
Turkish custom of drinking sweet mint tea from gold teapots at low
bronze tables. Then we proceeded to the hammam–the Islamic ver-
sion of the Roman baths. In accordance with Arabic cultural norms,
men and women are separated in the bath houses, so from start
to finish we only saw women, and those were the Parisian women
who were bathing with us in the pools and saunas, and the Arabic
women giving the massages.

Firstly, we were given black soap to lather on ourselves and told
to follow the step-by-step bathing routine, including a mud scrub,
steam rooms and ice plunges, until we ended up in a large domed
room where the communal massages were given. I had never had a
communal massage before and I certainly don't recommend it for
the bashful. Under the dome were a number of massage tables with
no sheets or towels or blankets and we had no option but to just lay
quietly on our designated tables side by side, stark-naked, awaiting
our masseuses.

Mine was a rotund Arabic lady wearing an apron and head cover
and she worked fast and furiously for about half an hour—so fast

and furious that there was to be no sleeping. What is it with Arabic masseuses and their fastness and furiousness? For the final part of the treatment I was asked to sit upright on the edge of the table with my legs dangling off the side and then my lady applied more oil on my chest and began massaging my breasts round and round and up and down. Wax on, wax off, wax on, wax off. Now, as I always say, I really am very open-minded but I must admit this took me by surprise. In French, I said to her that I too was a massage therapist and worked in New Jersey and that breast massage was not custom in the U.S. I explained that it was frowned upon and was considered intrusive, if not sexual.

She thought that was funny and said, "But why not? Feel good, no?" And she had a point; it really did feel good. And so, with no apology and without batting an eyelid, she continued in true Mr. Miyagi style in the Karate Kid movie: wax on, wax off, wax on, wax off…

Next door to France, in Germany, naked massages are the norm, too. As is naked bathing. Communal naked bathing. It's not for the faint of heart or the ultra-conservative.

I have to hand it to them: the Germans do relaxation right and believe whole heartedly in the curative effects of water and bath houses—*Kur Haus*. The government gives all German nationals a full six weeks off work every year to go to the *Kur Haus* and this is the right of every tax-paying citizen. Doctors prefer to prescribe a series of ten massages or ten *fango* mud pack treatments at the spa to treat stress rather than prescribing pills. So, a spa day is not a form of indulgent pampering reserved only for the rich and famous; it is for everyman's wellness and sanity.

During the time I lived in Germany, for the sake of my own wellness and sanity, I thought I'd give the *Kur Haus* a try. So, I headed to Baden-Baden to the world-famous Freidrichsbad Roman baths. Freidrichsbad was hailed as being the epitome of the old-world luxury Roman bathhouses and people came from all corners of the globe to be healed and relax in its curative waters. Just like the

German precision of the Porsche and the Mercedes-Benz, this spa also ran meticulously. Like everything else in Germany, there were rules—seventeen specific stages to be exact—that had to be followed in order.

And everyone had to be naked.

"Rule Number One" mandated that every person, without exception, must enter the spa unclothed, checking any self-consciousness or negative self-images at reception on their way in. There was no room for modesty or conservative attitudes.

I am liberal and free-spirited; I can do this…

Stage number one of the seventeen-stage ritual started in the all-female dry sauna, with me sitting in my birthday suit with all the other spa-goers who were wearing their birthday suits, too. I sat my bare butt on a marble slab in a dry heated room, where a sign recommended how many minutes I should stay there to achieve the full effect. After this, it was time to get my eight-minute soap-and-brush massage. It wasn't a massage so much as a pummeling with the therapist scrubbing so hard I feared he would take off every layer of skin leaving me red-raw. I don't know which was more painful though—the scrub, or lying on the table naked in front of my male massage therapist who I couldn't communicate with because he didn't speak English and I only spoke restaurant German! I could think of no appropriate pleasantries.

After my eight minutes of slight embarrassment, it was time to relax in a variety of steam rooms of different temperatures, followed by ice-cold water plunges. This might sound torturous, but going from an extremely hot environment to an ice plunge really is the most glorious feeling. My body tingled all over and I left feeling invigorated, yet relaxed at the same time. By this stage I didn't have a care in the world, and my stress had long gone. I'd even forgotten that I was naked amongst all the other women. But the next stage was co-ed.

Co-ed. All the German *damen* and *herren* and all the embarrassed tourists together in one giant bath—a multicultural soup!

Oh, this should be fun.

Too wiped out from the previous steps to care, I embraced my own bare body and the bare bodies of all the other strangers in the spa. I took the plunge, so to speak, and headed for the Roman pools in the domed center, Freidrichsbad's main attraction. In this domed room with its beautiful Roman architecture, I really got a feel for the history of the place and how it has stood the test of time for centuries. The marble pillars and the sunken baths took me back in time to Ancient Rome and I amused myself imagining Julius Caesar himself sitting next to me taking his weekly bath. They didn't bathe very often in those days.

I also smirked to myself watching the tourists all looking up pretending to be impressed by the ornate ceilings, avoiding eye contact with the other spa-goers. It was very quiet in there because the Germans abide by the *"ruhe bitte"* sign on the wall—silence please. I appreciated the quiet, and enjoyed the powers of the healing waters. The spa was so totally relaxing, I could barely put one foot in front of the other when I stood up to head to the last part of the ritual: the sleeping room.

The last sixteen steps had condensed me into a lump of delirious, incoherent putty and I was ready to be wrapped up in a cocoon for a welcomed nap. The sleeping room was quiet, complete with the now familiar *ruhe bitte* sign which, at this point was totally unnecessary because no one had the energy nor the inclination to speak anyway. It looked more like a hospital ward with rows of beds with everyone lying on top of sheets and blankets waiting for a member of staff to wrap them in swaddling clothes just like Moses. A plump German woman wrapped me tight, with my arms tucked in. I chuckled to myself thinking we must all look like an army of Egyptian mummies, but I didn't chuckle for very long because someone must have drugged me with lidocaine and I zonked out instantaneously. It seemed like a lifetime had gone by, but it was probably only two hours when I woke up naturally. I was reborn! Brand-spanking-new!

This seventeen-stage ritual had cost me only $50 which included the eight-minute $14 massage. And for over three hours of me time, my world-famous German spa experience would have been cheap at twice the price.

As a massage therapist, I feel that my indulgence in massages around the world is an investment in the self. It is research for my business, too. The experiences have made me a better therapist and my massages unique and eclectic. I cannot honestly say which country's style of massage I like best because there are benefits to all of them and it really does depend on my mood and demeanor—whether I want to fall asleep with scents of lavender or be beaten to a pulp with no mercy. I love the Zen-like ambiance when I go for a Japanese shiatsu but I also love the almost brutal Thai massages on the beach where I end up twisted into a sand-encrusted pretzel. And I love the fast and furious Arabic massages that leave me speechless and feeling like a well-pounded schnitzel. But I also enjoy the subtle healing from warm gentle hands in an energy massage like reiki, or treating my feet to a whole hour of reflexology. And I love being cocooned like Moses in the German spas of Baden Baden. I love it all, and for me, getting massages when I visit a new country is as important as tasting the food and drinking the wine: it's not pampering, it's experiencing culture and as such, it would simply be rude not to partake.

CHAPTER 10

Poker massage at the casino

"Life is not a matter of holding good cards, but of playing a poor hand well."

—Robert Louis Stevenson

*L*IFE WASN'T ALWAYS about getting pampered around the world; most of the time I was working in my office. After seven years of working in my first office in the tiny village in Germany, I moved to a slightly bigger office the other side of the pond in Marlton, New Jersey.

Neither my husband nor I wanted to leave Europe but we had no choice in the matter as it was time for a new military posting at McGuire Air Force Base, but New Jersey turned out to be instrumental in expanding my massage career.

The year was 2007 and alongside building a small part-time practice a few days a week, I got lucky enough to work in the five-star spa of one of the sexiest casinos in Atlantic City at the Jersey shore. To my amusement, this new spa job included probably the strangest experience of my profession: doing poker massage on the casino floor! My massage career has been anything but normal.

Along with the regular poker games in the casino, the hotel also hosted world-class poker tournaments which attracted hundreds if not thousands of players from all over the globe. The players consisted of 90% men wearing hoodies, baseball caps and very dark glasses, and 10% women who usually skipped the hoodies but donned dark glasses to hide their poker faces. These poker nuts with their poker faces would sit all day and all night at the tables, drinking coffee to keep them awake and in the game, while they competed for $100,000 in prize money.

Sitting hunched over the chairs at the gaming tables must have been quite uncomfortable, and no doubt caused suffering from numb bums and tight shoulders. Except, of course, for the players who were willing to partake in the massage deal conveniently available at their tables: $20 for a fifteen-minute rub-down.

There were three or four of us per shift doing the poker massage. Our job was to walk the huge ballrooms where the tournaments took place, with a pillow under our arms and massage oil in our pockets. Without disturbing the very serious business of gambling, we would ask if anyone at the table would like a mini massage. We had to hustle a bit but generally we would stay busy for our entire shift.

Many players opted for the minimum fifteen-minute basic tune-up for twenty bucks, but because it felt so good they would ask for another fifteen minutes. Some asked for an hour (which was the jackpot for us) but then I'd think to myself, *What exactly am I going to do for a whole hour while the guy is sitting slumped over his chair, cowboy-style?* I couldn't exactly turn him over like I would on a regular massage table, and there's not much you can do with the legs in that position, so creativity was a must.

The other problem was that these poker nuts were fully clothed so I had to do a shiatsu of sorts and squeeze the arms, and do some chopping up and down the legs and spend ages on the hands and fingers to pass the time. Everyone loved hand massages and I think it is perhaps one of the world's best kept secrets. People don't realize that having their palms and fingers massaged and stretched out is even more relaxing than a foot rub. And the best part about spending time on the hands, wrists and forearms meant I could kneel on my cushion on the floor so it was like taking a coffee break—except there was no coffee or any break because I still had to keep massaging. But at least it provided some sort of respite and took the monotony out of doing the same strokes.

I also changed things up by pulling out my forbidden little bottle of massage oil so I could throw in some relaxing Swedish moves, too. We weren't supposed to use oil because it stained the players' clothes but I paid no attention to the rules and took it only as a suggestion. It has always been my belief that rules apply but only sometimes and probably not to me.

If I know that I know better, then absolutely the rules do not apply to me and are simply to be ignored. I didn't agree with the no-oil rule because first of all, no one was wearing their Sunday best by any stretch of the imagination so they weren't going to ruin their fine garments. Secondly, it's tiresome to do pressure point massage for eight hours; we had to pull out all our stops. I would massage the neck and a bit of the shoulders with oil which would soak in leaving no evidence. I had full deniability and I could make that last a whole twenty minutes.

Tournaments where people planted themselves on chairs for days on end were a moneymaker for those of us working at the casino's spa. We could sign up in advance for extra shifts, including two shifts back to back, which made it an eight-hour work day. Even though we crawled out of there sometimes at two or three a.m., we would leave with pockets full of money. I was making $400 to $600 a day if I worked a double, so it behooved me to work myself into exhaustion.

Besides poker massage being a cash cow, it was also good because our work was relatively unsupervised. We could take breaks whenever we wanted. It was a shame that tournaments only happened a few times a year, because I liked the autonomy of it all.

There were two permanent positions doing poker massage on the casino floor at the hotel, and I was always watching to see if one opened up. Surprisingly, they were highly sought after. It was rumored that the girls who worked the floor were raking it in making an average of $1500 a week. A *week*! And both girls only worked four days. The reason the money was so good was that they made a straight commission cut–60/40 in their favor.

Such a cut is rare in the massage world, especially in fancy hotels. Most small places will pay 50% and if you can negotiate 60%, it's considered good pay. Poker massage, as funny as it sounds, was the most lucrative massage job to have in Atlantic City.

When the tournaments weren't going on, I worked in the casino's beautiful spa. Being a therapist at the most popular casino in Atlantic City, I felt I was at the top of my game. Novices fresh out of school were hungry to work in one of the big five-star hotels in New Jersey's answer to Las Vegas.

You'd think the pay was the driving factor but it really wasn't. And the standard wasn't even a 50/50 cut either. That would have been nice because the massages were $130, plus an obligatory 20% gratuity on top of that. It would have been nicer still if the tips went to us directly, but they were used as part of our salary. The way in which our pay was calculated was, let's say, very creative.

The creative remuneration started with a basic and measly $10 an hour which, for skilled, trained and licensed therapists, is pitiful. On top of that, the spa paid us a commission on the treatments we gave, which meant it was in our interest to talk our clients into a deep tissue or something fancy because the cut was higher. Something fancy meant a pricey milk and rose petal bath followed by a frou-frou aromatherapy massage in a private room.

We would get around a $25 commission for that as opposed to $17 if the client opted for a garden-variety Swedish massage. On top of our hourly rate and the commission, we received a percentage of the obligatory "tip." Altogether, that added up to about $35 an hour—barely 20% of the price of the treatment. Even more unpalatable was having to deal with the poor gouged clients who didn't know how the system worked and assumed we got the full tip saying, "I tipped you already. You get the 20% tip, right?" We would have to explain that it went to the corporation, not us. Some people would complain, but it never changed anything, and others would just whip out a $10 or $20 bill out of sheer pity.

So, what was the draw to work in such a casino where therapists only made 20%—probably the worst commission cut ever negotiated? Well, firstly it was the classiest casino in Atlantic City where all the beautiful people went, and secondly, working there was fun! We never sat around waiting for clients; we were almost always busy, which pretty much guaranteed we'd do at least five massages, sometimes six per shift.

Prestige also played a large part of it. There was always a chance that a high roller would drop us a $100 bill as a tip, or we'd find ourselves massaging some pop star or football player. Celebrities nearly always stayed at our hotel. On top of that, there was the promise of landing an in-suite massage gig in the $10,000 per night penthouse suites the size of a Manhattan loft. That's where the high falutin VIPs stayed. Ironically in an industry of gaming, we massage therapists were gambling on getting the best clients: the celebs and the big-tipping high-rollers.

But if truth be told, massaging celebs wasn't as glam as people might imagine. There is a specialty in the massage industry known as celebrity massage, whereby therapists work for an agency which deals exclusively with the rich and famous. My friend, Mimi, specialized in such a job. She would go backstage at concerts and set up, having to fit a six-foot massage table somewhere where there wasn't much privacy and the area was loud.

It was challenging for her to create a nice calming space with so much going on pre-show, but what was even more challenging was dealing with the spoilt, temperamental rock stars. She said they were a whole different kettle of fish and at times, massaging them was far from glam and a few had treated her abysmally.

To add insult to injury, Mimi had to pay for her own gas to drive two hours or more round-trip to make barely $100, after the agency took their cut, and who knew how much that was? So, the prestige of the job must be part of the salary because on that money and considering the infrequency and unreliability of the work, celebrity massage therapists would only make enough to buy cans of Chef Boyardee ravioli. And that is definitely not glam or sexy. Nonetheless, it was a great conversation piece at the bar.

"So, what business are you in?"

"Oh, me? Well, I am a massage therapist. But I only massage celebrities."

Whether I was working on celebrities or the average Joe, I was ecstatically happy being part of the team at the casino's spa. It was 2007 and I had been working as a massage therapist for exactly ten years. I felt as if I had hit the jackpot getting hired in Atlantic City, a popular gaming resort town since the 1930s.

It was even more of a dream job because I lived on our boat on my workdays, Friday through Sunday. Even though it was a hard slog on those three days, I still felt I was on vacation every weekend. I liked my three-day workweek.

Our boat was docked at the Trump Marina Casino and "I" Dock had been our second home for five years. Living on the boat felt like being on vacation at an all-inclusive resort complete with food and drinks flowing the entire weekend, thanks to our boozy boating buddies docked alongside our 27-foot sleep-aboard powerboat.

I had the best of both worlds. In the daytime, I would go sunbathing on the beach at Brigantine with my friends, or we would take the boat out and dock-and-dine for lunch on the bay. Then, I would wash off the salt and sand, and head to the spa. I worked diligently during my six-hour shift, and at ten p.m., I rushed back to the boat in time to hear the last set of the band playing on the deck.

Throwing all diligence and sensibility overboard, I tipped back fruity vodka cocktails till the wee hours with my boating friends, and danced to the live music. Our backdrop was the pristine palm trees swaying in the warm night's breeze, and the yachts rocking gently in the marina. Even though I was massaging for most of the weekend, it didn't feel like work at all.

My work day began at three in the afternoon when I picked up my uniform from Housekeeping on the way in, and it finished around ten at night when I returned my sweaty uniform on the way out. Someone to do my laundry: it was great! After changing into my uniform came the most fun part of the day: eating for free in the staff canteen with the other therapists and chatting and gossiping about some of the crazy things that had happened in the spa—who had massaged which celebrity, what they were like, who was staying at the hotel that weekend, how some sleaze-ball had had the audacity to ask for a happy ending from one of the girls. I mean, really? In a five-star hotel? It happened.

The staff canteen was much like a gourmet all-you-can-eat buffet on a cruise ship with long lines of employees. There were at least three soups daily, five kinds of pizza, a Chinese selection, an Italian section, a carvery with some kind of roast each day, a salad bar, a dessert bar, and an ice-cream machine. It was like being a kid in a candy store. It was also where most people put on about ten pounds during their first month of work—a bit like the "freshman fifteen" at university. Once we realized we were busting out of our uniforms, it was time to lay off the buffet.

We ate there twice a day: lunch at three before our shift officially started, and again at nine when our shift ended. It was gluttony at its finest! Contractually, we were only supposed to have one shift meal, but my hungry colleagues and I chose to take that merely as a suggestion.

We were also forbidden from taking food out of the canteen, but I disregarded that recommendation too and would shove a snack or two into my backpack. It was only a cake or two or some cookies to take back to the boat. And maybe an apple or an orange for breakfast. Sometimes a banana, too. And sometimes a couple of bread rolls for good measure. Perhaps a teeny bit of ham to make some sandwiches. But that was it, and I'm sure no one noticed; there was enough food there to "feed the five thousand."

Fortunately, there were not 5,000 massage therapists eating at the staff canteen, only about 65 of us. We all worked six-hour shifts, with 30 or so of us working on the spa floor at one time— an A and a B shift. The spa ran like clockwork with 30 treatment rooms plus some extra wet rooms.

Elegant flameless candles flickered inside the niches in the walls of our dimly lit spa rooms, while soft music enhanced the soothing atmosphere. A larger candle and one simple flower sat on a Balinese wooden tray atop a silk runner which matched our silk bedspreads. The rooms were dark, the atmosphere totally conducive to relaxation. This was my office; it calmed me and it was a pleasure to work in it. But the best and most luxurious room to work in was the Couples' Suite.

The Couples' Suite was a huge room like something out of a Beverly Hills mansion. The space included a Jacuzzi hot tub and a lounge area with a large flat screen television and it came stocked with fresh fruit, chocolates and champagne. It came with two massage therapists and was reserved for side-by-side massages and the price tag for all this pampering was a trifling $600 for 90 decadent minutes. Being assigned to the suite was a treat and a beautiful work environment. It was even better if you got to do the couples' massages with a friend. Then we could pull faces at each other and bang butts as we walked around the table, and try not to make each other laugh if the clients snored or farted. All this nonsense was taking place while the unsuspecting lovebirds lay zoned-out on heated tables with warm dry towels on their foreheads.

Couples could use the room as they pleased after their massages, but at ten minutes before the hour, we would turn off the jets from an outside switch and knock on the door signifying their time was up. Then the circus that was Operation Clean-up began.

Dirty sheets off the massage tables, clean sheets on, silky covers on top, candle on tray on pretty cover. Next, collect all wet towels, put chemicals in the tub and turn the jets back on. Don't forget to refill fruit bowl, and run like mad back to the main spa to see who was next.

It always amused me that there was so much mayhem and panic behind the scenes of an organization in the business of relaxation and calm. Looking at us, however, there were no signs of mayhem; we were professionals. If one of us ran behind, any other therapist could jump in and take the next client.

But if we were behind schedule, we were shooting ourselves in the foot because massages started on the hour and finished ten minutes before the top of the next hour. If someone else took our client, because we weren't running a tight enough ship, we lost an hour's pay so timeliness was key. And as we only had six hours per shift, the goal was to maximize the time, and get paid for all six hours by doing six massages.

The spa was a well-oiled machine and it was go, go, go, especially on the weekends. The hour massages were in fact only 50 minutes and from Minute 51 to Minute 59 we had to get the clients off the table, back in their robe, walk them to the locker rooms, sprint back to the room, throw the silk sheets down a big chute in the wall, grab clean sheets and make up the bed. This gave us a minute to pee, redo our lipstick and run to either the men's or the ladies' locker room to pick up the next person—all the while trying not to look frazzled and portray some semblance of control.

Sometimes the chaos was in trying to find the right client. We were given the names of our clients beforehand and, seeing a Jane Smith or an Anastasia Karloff on our list, we would naturally go to the ladies' locker rooms to pick them up. Or we'd see a Jose Perez or a Fred Jones and go to the men's locker room. But sometimes we would get a Chinese name—Min Fong for example. Well, was Min a boy or a girl? No one knew so it was a 50/50 shot and could take several trips back and forth before Min's sex was determined and the correct client picked up from the correct locker room.

If we were really unlucky, we had not one, but two foreign names on our schedule at the same time, and the running back and forth became an ill-timed workout. When this happened, we therapists wanted to slap the receptionists at the front desk for making a pig's ear of the scheduling.

In our five-star, world-renowned spa, along with the high rollers and celebrities we had other species of clients, namely the drunks and the trust-fund babies. And of the two species, the drunks were the least difficult to deal with. It was in the employee handbook that if guests were obviously inebriated we had the right to decline treatment. No one ever did because that would mean we would have no client, and no client meant zero *dinero*. Clients were asked to fill out a questionnaire of sorts, but the forms were completely useless and really only there for upgrades or to sell product at the end of the session. "Oh, you have sore shoulders. Might I suggest you opt for the deep tissue instead?" Or, "I noticed that your legs are very dry. Might I interest you in a very expensive cream?"

One of the questions on the client intake forms was, "Have you had any alcoholic beverages before coming to the spa?" No one ever checked yes but most of the hotel guests would gamble at the tables in the casino downstairs, taking advantage of the free drinks before coming for their massage. I'd say a huge percentage of our clientele had imbibed, and if we turned away every imbiber for having a little cocktail or three, the spa would have gone out of business a long time ago.

Dealing with tipsy clients meant that in addition to changing the sheets in between appointments, we would sometimes have to clean up a little pile of puke, or at least call Housekeeping to clean up the little pile of puke. And clean-up had to be completed in the Minute 51 to Minute 59 time-frame, otherwise the therapist would lose the room, the client and the pay.

Thankfully the trust-fund babies didn't usually leave the contents of their stomachs on the spa floor for us to clear up. Still, they were disgusting in plenty of other ways.

Trust-fund baby parents were inevitably "black card holders," which meant they were high rollers and treated like royalty and had everything comped. Their spawn took the phrase "sense of entitlement" to a whole new level. When they got bored of gambling away Daddy's pennies, they would saunter to the spa and demand massages, didn't care if they were late, expect it all to be on the house, and they never tipped.

These spoilt brats obviously didn't get the etiquette memo that says people are supposed to tip when something is comped, but who said money buys class? These precious gems who would boast obnoxiously, "I just blew twenty grand in one hand at the craps table, hahahaha…" could barely manage a thank you, let alone part with a twenty. When they were rude and intolerable there was nothing we could do. Or so we thought. Until one day when my coworker, Jason got sweet, sweet revenge on one of these specimens, and it was a delicious treat for all.

A trust-fund baby had booked a massage plus an add-on: the lime and coconut head massage which involves using aromatic tropical oils to massage the forehead and scalp. It's a sensuous aromatherapy treatment, totally indulgent and very relaxing. A good amount of oil is used and it gets in the hair so there is a trick to getting the oils out which the therapist is supposed to explain to the client afterwards. It is imperative to apply the shampoo to the hair immediately afterwards and under no circumstances wash it with water first. If the hair is rinsed with water first, it is almost impossible to get the heavy oils out, leaving it greasy, limp and unmanageable for days if not weeks.

From the time she entered the spa, a half an hour late, the trust-fund baby girl had been a little peach. She moaned that the therapist was male (there wasn't much Jason could do about that at this point) and she criticized the music playing, too. And the air-conditioning was too cold. And he wasn't going deep enough.

"I specifically requested a female", she grumbled.

Jason apologized that he wasn't a female. Smiling, he applied the aromatic coconut oil into her long strands of hair, rubbing it into her head. She demanded he change the music. He got up and obliged. Deciding he needed a little revenge, he did away with protocol and dumped the remainder of the tub of coconut oil on her head "as a treat" and finished off by wrapping her head in a warm towel. A warm and very *wet* towel.

"Now there is a trick to getting all the oil out of your hair, ma'am. Go straight into the shower and rinse the oils out with hot water first and let it rinse for a good ten minutes before applying the shampoo. Remember the water must be nice and hot. This will help make your hair silky and shiny."

Her hair would be drab, dull and lifeless for the foreseeable future. Oh, the perfection that is sweet revenge! Needless to say, he didn't get a monetary tip, but the psychic gratuity he received was huge. And getting his own revenge on behalf of all 65 massage therapists who had at least once been subject to bratty trust-fund baby behavior was priceless. I know all this because this was the kind of thing we talked about in the staff canteen.

I had been working at the casino for nearly six months and felt so lucky to be part of the massage therapy elite who worked in a five-star spa at the Jersey shore. But one Sunday night in October changed everything.

It had been a weekend of the usual celebs, drunks, trust-fund babies, back-to-back 50-minute massages, clients with androgynous names, and bellies full from overindulgence at the staff canteen. We were told that the spa was closing early and the entire staff was called to a meeting. This was completely unprecedented, and no one explained what was going on, but the meeting was mandatory and no one could leave.

Never mind that I might have a cocktail waiting for me at the

boat or that the band would be on their second set by now. I reluctantly stayed. The atmosphere in the break-room felt eerie—way
too quiet. None of the therapists looked at each other or spoke as
we awaited our fate.

It was 2008 and the economy had taken a nosedive, house
prices had plummeted, and people were getting laid off left, right
and center. A couple of our shift managers had been fired that
week, followed by the spa director. Highest paid, first to leave; isn't
that how it always goes? If that was the case, we therapists at the
bottom of the totem pole had nothing to worry about, because
apart from a bit of gluttonous behavior in the canteen worthy of
Mr. Creosote in the Monty Python sketch where his belly explodes
from overeating, we weren't actually *costing* the spa anything.

We sat in the break room on tenterhooks and in walked two
faceless big shots from upper management in their pinstriped, tai-
lor-made suits. The "meeting" was over almost as soon as it began.
It was a one-sided soliloquy delivered by Mr. Grossly Overpaid Big
Shot who harped on about the economy and the decline in the number of clients in the spa, and how the establishment had to let all 30
of us go. Not tomorrow. This minute. We, the entire second shift,
were fired *en masse* in one fell swoop and to add salt and lemons to
our fresh wounds the suits added, "Oh and you all officially don't
work here anymore so Security will escort you to Housekeeping to
hand in your uniforms. There will be no shift meal."

I was 50% shocked and 100% heartbroken and stood dumbfounded like everyone else. My girlfriends and I cried as we were
unceremoniously escorted out. I was still crying when my husband
picked me up.

He tried to console me, saying I didn't have to work, but I
still sobbed uncontrollably all the way home and chose to drown
my sorrows in copious gin and tonics. I was hungry and no shift
meal meant I had to eat leftovers in the fridge on the boat. It did
give me small comfort knowing I had stolen said leftovers from
the staff canteen the night before. Ha! That little bit of revenge

appeased me momentarily, until the realization that I was unemployed set in.

Now what was I going to do? Was my massage career over in this down economy? Was this a sign that it was time to finally get a real job? A grown-up corporate job? But after a decade of having fun massaging on my own schedule, wouldn't I be bored out of my gourd?

Over the next few weeks I did some soul searching in order to plan for my next move. Some of the other girls found work at other casinos and one landed a teaching gig at the National Massage Therapy Institute, NMTI. The one who became a teacher had only just graduated massage school three months earlier but she applied to teach nonetheless, and to her delight she was hired. Her leap of faith inspired me. Maybe I could teach, too?

I had always wanted to teach my trade, but was never confident enough. I wasn't sure if I was equipped with the correct academic ammunition, especially since I had trained in England and was working in America. I'd racked up thousands and thousands of massages over the years, and had been ready for a while to move on to the next step; I just didn't expect to be pushed overboard into hostile waters without a life jacket. But I was unemployed and had nothing to lose, so why not teach the wisdom of my years in the industry? I decided to apply. Just to see.

First, I needed to revamp my resume and do what everyone else does when going for a new job: exaggerate, embellish and flat out lie about experiences and qualifications. I sent in my doctored-up resume to about five schools along with a nicely written cover letter. And I waited.

It was the worst time in history since I could remember to embark on a new career. With the sub-prime market crashing and a new black President in power, things were unfamiliar and unsettled, people were losing their jobs and their lives were crashing like a deck of cards. The media reported story after story of families affected by the downturn in the economy and facing homelessness even when both parents had master's degrees.

It was a dire situation. Negativity and doom prevailed as people hunted for something that was becoming extinct: a good old-fashioned American job. With that in mind, I was more than surprised that my own search was fruitful.

One day a phone call came as I sat unemployed on my couch binge-watching old episodes of *Gordon Ramsey's Kitchen Nightmares*. A nice woman named Denise told me she was from NMTI. She asked if I was still interested in the teaching position at the Philadelphia campus and invited me in for an interview.

My potential new workplace was the cutest little school across the bridge from New Jersey, right next to Dunkin Donuts. It had a fast-growing student population and they needed a new teacher—yesterday. In the interview, I expressed concern that I may have forgotten a little of my anatomy and physiology over the years, but what I really wanted to say was, "Look, even if you paid me a million bucks I couldn't remember the first thing about any of the biology I learned, let alone teach it." But I kept my mouth shut, and they offered me the job. How lucky! How exciting! Although the image of the blind leading the blind did cross my mind.

So, with one door closing, another door had opened wide for me. And this door was my future—big, bright and shiny with a gold knob on it. I was going to be a teacher at a massage institute! No more rubbing drunken gamblers in a casino—I was upping the ante and entering the world of academia. I felt sophisticated and I would finally be using my brain. My headmistress and parents would be proud.

Take that, Atlantic City! Up your bum, as we say in England! Stuff your poker massage and your fancy celebs! And you can keep your free canteen food, too; it made me fat!

Clearly, I was no longer harboring any ill will at all, and there were certainly no hard feelings. Anyone could see I was over it and moving on like an adult. Still, I couldn't help but wish explosive diarrhea on the men in suits who fired us.

CHAPTER 11

Teaching the art of massage with Play-Doh

I DON'T KNOW WHY I was nervous about teaching something I had been doing as a career for so long. I had taught English before for seven years whilst living in Japan, so I knew how to teach, and I loved feeding a class full of knowledge-hungry students. I questioned my teaching abilities because even though I had studied all the massage-related anatomy and physiology years ago in my twenties for my original certification, I had aged a couple of years since then and probably killed off a few brain cells along the way overindulging in beer and fruity cocktails. I had to admit: even with twelve years in the business, when it came to the theory of my craft, I could hardly remember a thing. I had brain-dumped the lot and now I was in panic mode.

My new supervisor at NMTI knew I "needed a bit of a refresher course." Her solution was to feed me the class schedule day by day, page by page. She suggested I study just enough to teach the next day's class, and this I could manage. As long as I stayed even one day ahead of the schedule—24 hours, 1440 minutes—of what my students knew, I would be just fine and no one would know my dirty little secret.

To my relief, our strategy worked and if someone ever asked a question I didn't have the answer to, I would cleverly remark, "Well now, let's not get ahead of ourselves and dig into next week's material. We have enough information to process already from this week, wouldn't you agree?" They always agreed.

I enjoyed my new job. It was a job where I could be creative and where I had autonomy. I didn't merely lecture from a text book, I made classes interactive and fun. Preferring the kinesthetic teaching style where students learn by doing, I came up with the idea of learning through playing games: team games, ball games, card games, flash cards, and playing with Play Doh, and to my amazement, it was effective. Everyone was having fun while the information sunk in.

With the Play Doh, the task was to make muscles to scale and each group had to attach their muscle onto Bony Man, the life-size skeleton we had hanging in the front of the classroom. Sometimes we made the organs of the entire digestive system, including the esophagus, stomach, intestines and rectum. The rectum was unfailingly brown and big, and someone always put a tiny ball in the stomach. When asked what the tiny ball was, they said it was a cheeseburger or a donut. And just for that I would get them to explain the digestion of a Big Mac and which enzymes in the mouth broke down the beef and cheese, and which broke down the buns. I didn't mind that they were silly, as long as they learned too.

Learning with squelchy goo was fun but I had a dilemma. Sometimes it was a small dilemma and sometimes it was a large one. It didn't matter what I asked the students to make: muscles, tendons or the alimentary canal—someone always made a penis. Without fail, in my class of adults, there was always some clown who felt the need to sculpt the male anatomy. I would walk around the class to check that they had done the work correctly, and there it was, lo and behold: a penis, complete with dangling gonads. Their cheeky faces anticipated my reaction which would usually be, "Ah yes, the male anatomy. We are making these again in Chapter 22, so well done children, you are ahead of the game!"

I loved the group projects and the games we played, my favorite being Jeopardy. Playing Jeopardy served as a review tool at the end of each module. Reading the definitions out loud twice reinforced the new and sometimes complicated vocabulary. Best of all, because the students thought we were just mucking about playing games, they didn't see it as studying and they processed the information more readily.

It was fun, but who would have thought that questions on the human body could create such fighting and heckling when a team member got the question wrong? Luckily, the banter on both sides was done in jest, and it was a win-win even though a few over-achievers got bent out of shape.

With the games came prizes too, and they were usually of the chocolate variety. I threw mini bars of Snickers and Twix across the classroom to all the winners and, at the end of the school day, students left on a high—educational and sugar.

I left on a high, too. I felt that I was doing something purposeful and I was fulfilled seeing a new generation of massage therapists eager to learn. I saw how the interactive games promoted class bonding, social skills and self-confidence—qualities which were very much needed with a student body from the inner city. I felt like I was making a difference in their lives and giving them something to be passionate about.

There was value in what I was doing. I wasn't just rubbing people back-to-back all day long in a spa or painting anti-aging vitamin masks on their faces; I was educating. Students were grasping what I taught, and it reflected in their high grades. I was proud to bring over a decade of worldly experiences to the table and students seemed to enjoy hearing my stories from other countries. Unlike so many times before during my career, I felt respected. No one was trying to expose themselves on my table or ask what

I wanted to do when I grew up. Everyone around me appreciated the value of touch.

I looked forward to going to work in the mornings and most days began with hugs as students walked through the doors. This took me a while to get used to but massage school is not like any normal educational institution—it's very touchy, feely. Being an instructor was not only my job but my source of amusement from Monday to Thursday from nine until three, and amidst the hard work and the required exams, there was much laughter and banter.

I usually started the day with the theory of massage therapy— the anatomy and physiology. Sometimes the subject was complicated, especially the nervous system. It was a rather unpalatable cocktail of physics and chemistry and even when broken down, the information was received by the students with tilted heads and muddled looks on their faces. It required full attention and we instructors used to tell our students to "bring their 'A' games" during this, the most difficult module of the curriculum. Many students took notes, some highlighted the textbook, while others took a more unexpected approach to learning.

Tiffany's unique approach to learning was gazing into her pink Hello Kitty compact mirror and applying strawberry-flavored lip gloss as I lectured, and it seemed that the less she understood, the more lip gloss she applied. Furthermore, she had the audacity to sit at the front of the class as she did this. Not only was she disturbing her classmates; she was disturbing me!

"So, the electrical impulse travels along the neuron via the axon…Tiffany, do we really think that reapplying one's lip gloss is the most productive thing you could be doing right now? Is this helping you understand the material? Hmm? Maybe take some notes?" I suggested, handing her a sheet of paper and a pen. Drawing a diagram on the board, I continued my lecture.

"When the impulse reaches the dendrites, it jumps across a synapse and connects to the next nerve cell to continue the muscle contraction…"

I looked around. Tiffany was doodling.

"Tiffany, it doesn't seem that you are focusing on this at all. It seems that you are now doodling, and doodling isn't going to enhance your massage career, is it?"

My reprimands were met with attitude—rolled eyes and loud sighs. The eye-rolling, I could deal with but not the next little stunt she pulled some weeks later.

It was mid-winter, cold with snow on the ground and most students kept their hoodies and coats on as the heating was slow to kick in in the mornings. I wondered why the fluffy pink pea-coat she had come in with was hanging on the back of her chair and why she kept rolling her sleeves up and down, and I also wondered why she kept looking at her knees and seemingly fiddling with her underpants. Soon it became clear: she had the answers written in pen on her forearms from her wrists to her elbows and all the way up her leg from her knees to the top of her thighs and astonishingly under her waistband, too. It was right there and then she received her first written warning.

Teaching moment: do not cheat in class.

Tiffany wasn't the only student with a unique way of learning. Jeff learned by sleeping, and the information seeped in through osmosis; it was quite spectacular.

Jeff was a man of many talents. A balding guy in his forties with a moustache and a constant grin on his face, he could sleep while massaging, sleep while standing, nod off half way through a conversation, and he could even fall asleep during his lunch and land in his sandwich before he fully regained consciousness. His talents were indeed unique and provided the class with much laughing fodder. And being a jokester, Jeff often made fun of his own mishaps.

One afternoon, to finish off the school day, I divided the class into two teams for a rapid-fire quiz. It was fast paced, people were on the ball in competitive mode, determined to win the cheap candy I had bought as prizes for the winning team.

"What is the longest, strongest bone in the body?"

"FEMUR!"

"What are the upper chambers of the heart called?"

"ATRIA!"

"What are the antagonist muscles to the rhomboids?"

"THE PECS!"

"What is the…What is everyone laughing at?"

They all pointed to Jeff who had been propping himself up against the whiteboard. We stood in amazement as we witnessed him slipping followed by buckling at the knee. Who buckles at the knee in class? This jolted him for a split second and he lifted himself up once more. Still leaning on the board, the cycle resumed: slipping, slipping some more, buckling at the knees, brief awareness of the classroom but then more shut-eye. We were all bursting at the seams in an attempt to suppress our laughter but it was when Jeff's knees buckled for the last time waking him up in mid-crash that we all lost our composure. The hard floor woke him up; fortunately, he wasn't hurt. And he did see the funny side, especially when he saw the rest of the class red-faced laughing at his expense. I probably shouldn't have joined in.

All joking aside, I was concerned about him. What on earth was going on? It crossed my mind that he might be unwell or have some serious disease like narcolepsy—the chronic neurological disorder where people suddenly fall asleep in mid-conversation or on the job. That might explain things.

After dismissing the class, I took him aside and expressed my concerns. He made a big joke out of it and said that no, he didn't have narcolepsy and it was just strong pain meds that he sometimes needed when his back pain became unbearable, and they had a tendency to zap his energy. He promised he would go to bed earlier and try to stay awake in class. Then added, "I know you think I am sleeping but I am listening; the information enters my brain through osmosis! But, I will try not to fall asleep in class again."

And he did try. But alas, he failed.

At the end of the month during the practical evaluation, Jeff was working on one of his classmates. He was being graded on technique, on his posture, form and on timing. I watched from a distance and wrote notes on his grading sheet. He stopped on one spot. It's normal procedure in bodywork. It is called ischemic compression and is used when a tough knot is found in the muscle. You hold the point, temporarily interrupt blood flow, and when you release the hold, the blood whooshes through the muscle bringing fresh oxygen and nutrients and hey presto, the adhesion is unblocked.

Good man, Jeff! So, he was listening and now applying the theory to the technique.

Except the therapist isn't supposed to close his eyes, and head-bobbing isn't part of it either. But there it was: eyes a-fluttering, head a-bobbing and pig-like snorts coming from the mouth. Most unprofessional and absolutely not any massage move I have ever seen.

Somewhat amused I continued to observe; teaching bodywork was free entertainment and great material for the teachers' lounge after school. I watched his head droop lower and lower into his chest. He stood motionless—fast asleep, his hands still on his client's back.

I was stifling a giggle and then I realized half the class was snickering watching him, too. I shouted, "Jeff!" and he stood upright, startled with an "oh no, not again" expression. I had no choice but to give him a zero on the test and he failed his practical exam. The same thing happened the following month when I was grading him on foot Reflexology, and when I noticed his squashed nose resting on his client's big toe, I shouted, "For God's sake... Jeff!" Another zero.

The man did have quite a sense of humor and unlike Tiffany, I didn't want to throw him out of school because he was such a likeable rogue. During break times, he would tell far-out stories that had the whole class in hysterics. Whenever we finally stopped laughing at his whopper of a tale, he loved to add, "That would be funny, if it weren't true." Another uproar of hysteria would ensue. I had to hand it to him; he knew how to keep us entertained and all the students liked him. I liked him too, and enjoyed having him in my class.

I think the afternoons were my favorite part of the day, when it was time to put our theory into practice and I could see how the students were developing into real-life therapists. The practical classroom was set up with royal blue massage tables lined up in a row, and the students wearing matching blue scrubs were partnered up at each one. One afternoon shortly after I got hired, I was demonstrating a new move and the whole class was gathered around in the center. It was a myofascial release move called skin-rolling where you pick up the skin and roll it out, almost peeling it off the bone. It's a little painful, but effective in getting rid of toxins.

I asked for a demo model and Allan, a tall lanky guy in his twenties, volunteered and jumped up on the table. It was challenging for me to pick up the muscle tissue as he was so skinny. I remarked, "Allan, would you please fatten yourself up a bit for next time? There's more fat on a chip," at which the whole class erupted with laughter. Everyone paired up and went to practice this new move, and as I watched them work I thought everything was going swimmingly. I was mistaken.

I had partnered Allan up with Louise, one of our more mature students who had decided to take up massage therapy as a hobby in her retirement. She was new to the school and was finding some of the basic massage strokes hard to follow, but I remained hopeful that she would soon adjust. Maybe today was the day?

As the students practiced, I hovered over each table testing them on the names of the muscles they were palpating. I asked Tiffany, my strawberry lip-gloss student, but she had no idea. I tried a simpler question.

"So, Tiffany, as massage therapists, are we massaging muscles or bones do you think?" This was the most ridiculous and basic of questions from the first day of school.

Flicking her blonde hair and licking her red lips, she responded with, "Umm...wellllll..."

"Well, what?" I prompted.

"I'm gonna sayyyy...BONES!" she finally announced, looking proud of herself.

The whole class roared with laughter—even the ones who were pretending to be asleep. It was at this point that I gave up and sincerely hoped she had a Plan B because massage therapy just wasn't working out for the poor girl.

Tiffany wasn't the only person having difficulty that afternoon. It appeared that Louise couldn't quite grasp the skin-rolling technique; instead she had unfortunately grasped something quite different. After class was dismissed, Allan, her partner, ran up to my desk and nearly knocked me over.

"Don't make me work with Louise again," he pleaded. "She was all up in my junk!"

"What do you mean, 'up in your junk?'" I really wasn't down with the Philly lingo yet.

"She was massaging my hamstrings and then just grabbed my...you know...junk!"

It was clear that I was going to have to talk to Louise face to face, and I wished this wasn't part of my job.

When I carefully broached the subject the following morning, Louise was quite taken aback at the accusation of touching Allan's private parts and genuinely had no idea that she had done anything wrong, insisting she hadn't touched any "junk" at all. She blushed, was truly embarrassed and genuinely apologetic. I believed it was an innocent, if not naïve, mistake and I could only conclude that she may need to review the geography of the male anatomy north of the hamstrings.

In practical class we tried to create as much of a spa atmosphere as possible by circulating lavender and sandalwood essential oils through a diffuser, and in doing this we all received a therapeutic daily dose of aromatherapy. It seemed to keep everyone calmer and more focused, myself included. But on one hot summer's afternoon and with a new batch of recruits, I couldn't help but notice that the aromatherapy had been replaced by a new strange smell and it was far from therapeutic.

As I was supervising, I detected a foul stench. Was it the drains? Was something dead and rotting at the back of the room? If I had to guess, I'd say that it wasn't, in fact, a dead animal but an acute case of butt or ball sweat. Or maybe feet. Cheesy feet of the fermented Gorgonzola variety.

Armed with my steaming hot coffee held close to my face so I could inhale the vanilla fumes of my latte, I ventured cautiously over to the source of the odor. I stopped at Jen's table. She was working on Nicky's calves.

"Jen, are you getting the hang of stripping the muscle fibers?" I asked, putting my coffee down so I could help guide her thumbs. But it seemed that muscle stripping was the least of her worries.

"Mandy, she stinks so bad, it's making me feel sick," she whispered in my ear.

Funny because I was thinking the exact same thing.

Jen added, "I don't care if you send me home. I'm not working with Nicky ever again."

I replied, "But Jen, she likes you and she listens to you. Do you think you could maybe broach the subject and hint that she needs to shower and put her scrubs and her sheets in the laundry at least once a week?" And with a smile I added, "I will give you ten bucks."

She looked at me half smiling and with her mouth wide open about to respond when I cut her off. "Alright, alright, you drive a hard bargain; I will up my bribe to twenty." We both smiled knowing full-well I was joking. I sighed and said, "Don't worry, I will sort this out." I couldn't argue with Jen as I, myself, would have refused point blank to work with her pungent partner.

Something needed to be done. Jen wasn't the only one who had refused to partner up with her unwashed classmate. Mike had tried to bribe me with coffee and my favorite peanut butter Twix and I'm embarrassed to say it had worked for him. Some would say I am easily corrupted but I feel that's a tad unfair. And considering it was for chocolate and not for money, it wasn't technically corruption in the true sense of the word. But in all truth, I had a genuine problem; everyone had caught on and was bringing in Twix bars and my staple vanilla lattes from the coffee shop next door in the hope of getting out of working with Nicky. It was time for my supervisor's help.

After my conversation with Jen, I excused myself for a bathroom break and went to have a little chat with Denise on the subject of B.O. and the likes. I told her that the stench in the classroom of late had been permeating the entire space and that many of the students had started to complain. Denise seemed unfazed as I explained the predicament. As a supervisor, she had obviously been through this dilemma before and asked matter-of-factly,

"Is it Vagodor"?

"Yes, Denise. I am afraid it is."

Vagodor was a term that we teachers had made up in the staffroom as a joke but, unfortunately, it was serious and we had to address the very awkward, unspeakable subject of odor coming from the vagina: a vag-odor, if you will. It was shocking that some students didn't bathe before coming to school or seemingly didn't bathe at all for that matter. We devised a plan that in one-hour Denise would come into the class saying I had an urgent phone call and she would take over and subtly visit the issue. I was off the hook. Oh, thank the Lord! Publicly discussing Vagodor was not in my job description and was way above my pay grade.

Back in the classroom, Denise tactfully broached the subject as I listened from the other side of the door.

"I just came to see how you are all doing so far, and it looks like things are going great!", she began. "But isn't it hot and sweaty in here? And, dare I say, a little…smelly? I know it's over 90 degrees outside and we all get sticky at times in the summer, but we do have to be more cognizant of our personal hygiene in the classroom. Because I am noticing some body odor in here that isn't so fresh."

There were comments and some snickering and I am sure at this point most of the class realized who she was talking about.

Denise continued. "No one wants to work with sweaty, stinky partners. I shouldn't need to say this, but all students must shower before they come to school and make sure their uniforms are washed regularly. And let's not forget to be generous with our deodorant. Everyone with me?"

I hoped everyone was with her and that Nicky would take the hint. She didn't. She remained unwashed all the way to graduation day and air freshener became our only saving grace.

Apart from a few students who tested my patience, I felt like we were one big cheerful family. I was in my element being in the classroom and I bloomed in my new job as an instructor. Teaching finally felt like I had a real job.

Students were grasping what I taught and it reflected in their performance. They were thriving and I was fulfilled seeing them share my love of massage therapy. The school was a relatively stress-free workplace and my work colleagues—the other teachers—were awesome, all with a wicked sense of humor which kept us laughing every day. Our school was a happy, fun place to be. It was the most rewarding job I'd had in my entire life and I felt that I could be content teaching forever.

In a vocational school in Philly, I had truly found my own vocation.

CHAPTER 12

Energy massage and the uninvited poltergeist

"Sci-fi has never really been my bag. But I do believe in a lot of weird things these days, such as synchronicity. Quantum physics suggests it's possible, so why not?"

—John Cleese of Monty Python

MY FAVORITE LESSONS were during the last module of the curriculum, where we talked about traditional Chinese medicine, spiritual healing and the power of energy massages.

Anyone who loves massage would have probably tried such energy work as shiatsu, reiki, Healing Touch, chakra healing or even polarity. To the lay person, these massage modalities could best be described as faith healing or the laying on of hands. In the most basic of terms, it is like massaging the invisible. Why the invisible? Because it works in the aura, the body's electro-magnetic field, rather than on the physical body itself.

Given that energy is an invisible phenomenon, it is difficult for most people to fathom. But we can feel it—especially as massage therapists—and it's not unusual for us to pick up on our client's energy. By this, I mean we can very easily take on their emotions or even their ailments. It's not that we possess any special powers; the lay person can feel energy too, even though they might not realize it.

How? It's the feeling everyone has undoubtedly experienced being around a person who is a naysayer, moaning all the time. We tend to feel bad when we are around these people and that is because their negative energy is bringing us down. We are picking up on their energy. Consequently, we don't want to be near them.

Similarly, when we are around happy, positive people we feel good; their positivity rubs off on us and lifts our spirits. Positive or negative, energy rubs off. It is contagious just like chickenpox and Ebola.

I had dabbled in some energy work in the Healing Touch class I took in Holland during my first year in practice, but it wasn't until I massaged Jill that I fully comprehended just how powerful energy could be. It was only my second year in the business when a very weird thing happened.

Jill was a petite but strong high-ranking linguist in the military, who loved deep tissue massages. She was one of those clients who would always say, "Go as deep as you can, you can't hurt me." As usual, I used my elbows to give deep pressure, but half-way through she reacted badly and seemed to be having a panic attack. She sat bolt upright gasping for air and said she felt dizzy. I immediately stopped the session and asked what was wrong. Breaking out into a sweat, she struggled to get her words out.

She looked at me with terror in her dark eyes as she nervously twisted her curly brown hair. "I was right back at the car accident with my brother, five years ago," she said. "You won't believe this but I could smell the burning rubber and it felt like I was inhaling the fumes from the car and I couldn't breathe." She rubbed her trembling hands over her tiny thighs.

I did believe her. Science has an explanation for this; it's called *regression* whereby the mind goes right back to the time of the accident or trauma, and the person relives the moment, play by play. Consciously, we may not remember, but our cells do. It's called *cellular memory* and sometimes bodywork can trigger the trauma. It is a difficult concept for some people to accept, but that pain in the shoulder, lower back, hips or stomach could very well be repercussions of an accident, a break up, or any other particularly traumatic time in a person's life.

When it comes to energy massage, another strange enigma is that the body never forgets its amputated limb. It is something that I've dealt with only a few times in my career and as odd as it sounds, when I am massaging the body of an amputee, I can still feel the energy of the missing limb. I feel a tingling, a warmth, a fuzziness in the aura, and the person who has lost the leg can also feel that "something is still there." The energy—the blueprint of the limb—still remains, and trained massage therapists can feel it. It's called the *Phantom Limb Phenomenon* and it still blows my mind when I am feeling something that is not physically there.

To many people, when I talk about energy, it sounds like I'm crazy. I am not. My friends know I am not crazy or lying or making up these stories, but even they find them hard to grasp. For them and for many others, energy is what they get after a cup of strong Columbian espresso in the mornings or after a brisk walk or run. This is why, at massage school, we saved this material until the very last module. It is unconventional and requires some thinking outside of the box.

In my second year of teaching at NMTI and a full twelve years into my practice, I set out to teach the much-anticipated energy module to another set of students. Like so many of my graduates before them, they were apprehensive and protested, bemoaning that it was a waste of time studying energy massage when they were never going to practice it; it wasn't their thing. But this was their last module before graduation and if they failed it, they would fail the entire program. I suggested they all pay attention, be open-minded and learn something new, lest they didn't want to graduate and work in Walmart.

I started with baby steps, explaining about energy fields, that we have an electromagnetic field or aura around our bodies. Most of the class had at least heard of auras before. I asked if they had ever met anyone for the first time and got "bad vibes" or if they ever felt a kind of magnetic attraction to someone. Had they ever felt a person was standing too close to them in the supermarket and they were "in their space?" All this, they could relate to, so that was a good start.

Then I explained that just like we have an electromagnetic field, we also have seven energy centers called *chakras* which are like spinning wheels going through our bodies. This information was met with blank looks and raised eyebrows, but I think I pushed them over the edge when I mentioned that in practical class we would be learning how to pick up the energy of the spinning chakras on other people. With pendulums.

"Pendulums like what witches use?" one of my suspicious male students in the back of the class asked.

"Yes, Smurf. Exactly." Smurf just happened to be one of the most skeptical in the group.

I had bought about ten wooden pendulums made out of rose wood and I gave out one per pair of students. Many energy workers use crystals to pick up the energy from the chakras, but rose wood is light and picks up the energy better, so it is much easier for beginners to use. I demonstrated how to use the pendulum on Smurf by having him lay face-up on the table while I held it dangling on a string about six inches above his body over each chakra, each energy center.

I started from the root chakra. I pointed to its location in between the thighs and held the pendulum right below Smurf's buttocks for a couple of seconds. It quickly picked up his body's vibration and started spinning clockwise, drawing a big circle all by itself.

"You're twirling that string in your fingers", someone commented from the back.

"I am absolutely not, I swear. Why would I lie to you? It's not me, it's Smurf's own energy," I argued.

"Swear on your life!"

"I swear on my Bernese mountain dog's life."

And that's all it took to convince them that it was energy from the chakras and not me; they knew how I loved my dog, Cheyenne, more than anything in the world.

I continued my demonstration, testing each of the seven chakras located in between the legs, below the belly button, above the belly button at the sternum, the heart, the throat, in the middle of the forehead and above the head. When one was out of balance, the pendulum spun in an anti-clockwise direction or just rocked from side to side indicating an imbalance, which in turn suggested a physical or emotional problem in the body. In such case, I showed the students how to rebalance the body by putting their hands on the client gently and letting the "warmth" of their hands penetrate. It was a totally new and very different style of massage for them, and one which required subtlety and concentration. Miraculously, when I concentrated the power of my hands and set good healing intentions as if in meditative prayer, the pendulum started to spin clockwise when retested. Healing 101.

Armed with their new wooden tools, the 20 students who made up my class began to experiment. Each student partnered up, and ten groups of students in their blue scrubs worked on ten blue massage tables set up adjacent to each other. I drew the curtains and made the room dark. The only light flickered from burning candles—the grounding and calming aroma of frankincense permeating the space. Healing music played softly in the background, carefully selected for its sounds of crystal healing bowls and gongs vibrating to resonate with the seven chakras.

I looked around the class at the pendulums swinging to and fro and drawing huge circles as they picked up the body's energy.

There were smiles of satisfaction on faces, open mouths, and raised eyebrows in disbelief that they were actually doing this. Receiving this kind of treatment was very relaxing so most of the partners laying on the tables were asleep. Those who remained awake had their mouths open too, no doubt fascinated by the spinning above their foreheads from their third eye chakras. The peace and tranquility were disturbed only by the excited shrieks of students.

"Whoa, that's so cool!" and "Look, I'm not doing anything, this wooden thing is really picking up your energy."

Even the skeptics like Smurf who slid off the table feeling better, lighter, and completely relaxed, seemed to be embracing the new phenomenon. After a short afternoon of practice, every single student in the class was picking up energy and acknowledged they were indeed not moving the pendulums themselves; rather it was the other person's own electromagnetic field that made them spin. They were really into learning about energy and that was indeed cool!

"See, you are all doing it; you are all picking up energy," I said proudly. "This, my friends, is what I was talking about. This is the essence of healing."

After they embraced this new skill and opened their minds a little, they were excited for the much talked-about Reiki Day where a professional reiki master came to be our guest speaker and do a demonstration for the whole school. I say demo but it was actually more like a magic show with smoke and mirrors in a quest to prove the power of energy. I had attended a demo by the same master before and it was fascinating.

For special occasions, all four classes assembled in one of the large classrooms where we taught the practical classes and on that day, we included the intro class who had only been at our school for a week. We positioned the blue tables around the perimeter of the room for everyone to sit on. About a hundred eager faces all looked onto the one massage table in the middle of the floor and at the reiki master, Ricky, a petite woman in her forties with a brown bob and a clean, make-up free face. She had been practicing reiki for nearly ten years and she understood the workings of energy better than anyone I knew in the field.

She liked to make her demos spectacular and brought with her some interesting props: crystal singing bowls, crystals pendulums and giant gongs which added a weird mystical atmosphere to the whole show. To begin the demonstration, she spread out her hands and announced dramatically, "I don't know what issues might come up because we are working with energy and spirit. There might be tears or laughter or even anger. I may receive messages from loved ones who have passed on to the spirit world. "

She asked for a volunteer from the audience and Keisha jumped at the chance. Keisha was the class diva—a vivacious and striking black woman with long black wavy hair and trademark false eyelashes. She batted those lashes at her male peers in practical class when she wanted to receive massage first rather than give, and she rolled her eyes when she didn't get her way. I liked her; her antics amused me, and she was full of spirit. I am sure she only volunteered to be the demo thinking she was in for a nice massage or even better, a nap. She hopped up on the table, lay face up and closed her eyes. 200 eyeballs stared at her, waiting to see what would happen next.

Little did they know, something terrible was about to happen.

True to form, Ricky started with dramatic effects by striking her giant gong for a loud vibration which permeated the room. Then she explained that with her crystal pendulums, she was going to begin testing how Keisha's chakras were spinning to see where her energy blockages were, just like we had done in class. By the eager, excited looks on my students' faces, I could see they were all-in.

We all watched in silence and the only noise was the diminishing sound of the gong. Suddenly the room felt cold and I shivered. The temperature seemed to have dropped dramatically and the chill gave me tiny goosebumps. *It must just be the air conditioning kicking in.*

Ricky quietly asked Keisha, now almost asleep, if she had any physical problems. She shook her head but then quickly corrected herself, "I do sometimes get anxiety pangs in my chest, but it's nothing really."

Ricky nodded as she struck her white crystal singing bowl, moving it ceremoniously down Keisha's body back and forth from her head to her toes as it made a kind of humming sound. This, she explained, was the crystal bowl giving off energy vibrations.

Vibes. Even the novices from intro class got it when she said vibes. Ricky then took her jade pendulum and began swinging it over the seven chakras of the body waiting for it to pick up the energy and spin. But it stopped abruptly at the heart chakra and proceeded to rock back and forth signifying a blockage. Ricky took a deep breath and closed her eyes as if meditating or in prayer, then put her warm hand over Keisha's heart for what seemed like a good ten minutes.

We all sat mesmerized, focusing on the pendulum swinging more and more violently. I assumed at this point it was probably negative energy coming out, but I wasn't entirely sure; it wasn't what normally happened. All 100 students' gazes fixated on the angry pendulum and on Keisha. Just then, she started convulsing on the table.

A few people laughed. Perhaps they thought this was just part of the show, that she was faking. I thought the same thing. But she wasn't.

Things were going horribly wrong.

I would never have believed the tale I am about to tell had I not watched it happen. It was something that I am sure none of us in that room that day will ever forget. However much we wanted to.

Keisha's convulsions continued and she seemed oblivious, unconscious. This wasn't an act. I looked around and saw fear in the student's eyes, a few clutching each other. Suddenly, we all heard a loud scream.

It came from one of the students—the quiet red-head in the back. She darted toward the bathroom in the corner of the room, her face white and withdrawn. She locked herself in and refused to come out, screaming, "He's in the mirror and won't leave me alone!"

Another scream came from a girl at the back of the class, Suzie. This blood-curdling scream tore out from Suzie's mouth, and in what looked like a fit of hysteria, she ran out of the classroom into the parking lot.

Is this a joke? Are these two in cahoots? Have the little shits planned this just to disrupt the class? If this is a prank, it's not funny at all.

Ed, my co-worker, ran outside after her. Through the classroom's large picture window, I watched him kneel on the ground, rubbing her back, trying to calm her down. Just like Keisha, Suzie began convulsing, flapping on the ground.

What the hell was going on?

Things were spinning way out of control and I was ill-equipped to deal with it.

I'd had enough of the reiki demo. It was like a horror movie I wanted to slam off, or quickly change the channel. Couldn't we stop, call it a day and send the students home early?

The drama continued outside. I heard Ed yell for the reiki master to come out to the parking lot and help. Ricky ran to the door, leaving me to calm down Keisha and supervise the class. What I wanted to say was, "Wait! Don't leave me here!" I was feeling anything but calm; my throat was dry and my chest felt tight. What I actually said was, "Now guys, everybody keep calm and don't panic! I am sure Ricky has this under control. If you could all just stay sitting."

But the little buggers were already running to the window *en masse* to see what was going on; they wanted front row seats to the train wreck.

Inside, Keisha stopped jerking and fell into what appeared to be a peaceful sleep. I gave her a reassuring squeeze on the arm, then ran to the window too. To supervise of course. Well I had to, I was the teacher.

Most of the class stood at the window, some with their faces squashed against the glass. The others stood on chairs to get a better view. Some remained seated, too frightened to move.

The next thing we saw was horrifying, defying all explanation. We had stepped into the movie-set of Poltergeist.

Suzie wailed from the depths of her lungs as she lunged forward. "I'm going to kill her," she cried. "Get him out of me!" As if this wasn't macabre enough, she spoke in two entirely different voices just like in the horror movie.

Two distinct voices and pitches bellowing out of one mouth. Ed and four others attempted to confine her, but to no avail. She fought with the strength of Goliath, broke away, and charged at the window, terrifying all of us on the other side.

We looked on in shock as she tried to crawl her way up, clinging to the metal on the window with what appeared to be superhuman strength until the five men finally managed to restrain her. Just then, without warning, she passed out and dropped to the ground. We watched in disbelief as her eyes went black like a shark and she foamed at the mouth.

Even the reiki master who had presumably seen it all, stood frozen taking in the horrific scene, her arms slack at her sides, her mouth wide open in shock. The men moved away and she cautiously approached Suzie. At that, Suzie leapt back up and lunged at her with full force, threatening in a deep male voice, "I AM GOING TO KILL YOU!"

The men rushed forward to help, but Ricky motioned with her hand for everyone to stay back. "It's OK, he wants me...it's me who he wants," she announced calmly.

I'm sure I wasn't the only one thinking, *He? Who in the hell is "he?"*

To say we were all freaked out at this point by these ghoulish events, would be a gross under-statement. Had a real evil spirit taken over Suzie's body? It was a ridiculous notion but I had to ask myself, *Was she really possessed?* It was beyond irrational; it was crazy!

Just then, Ricky put her hands on Suzie and appeared to be saying something. For now, all was calm outside. But inside, Keisha started to convulse again. It appeared that when Keisha rested, Suzie raged, then when Suzie became calm, Keisha violently shook. It went back and forth like this between the two girls like a see-saw for a good ten minutes.

It was official: it had to be a superhuman phenomenon because what was happening defied all rationalization. I certainly couldn't even begin to explain it and it seemed none of us could do anything to stop it. There was no hiding from our students that the staff was just as terrified as they were, and we all stood together frozen, helpless.

Amidst the pandemonium, someone must have called an ambulance. Medics arrived in time to find Suzie convulsing again on the sidewalk. They tried to restrain her and lift her on to the stretcher, but through the struggle, she kicked one of the medics in the balls. Hard!

After more struggling she passed out again and lay still long enough for the medics to load her into the waiting ambulance. My supervisor, Denise, was now at the scene. Probably because she was also a nurse, she was allowed to ride along.

Back in the school building, the remaining students watched as the ambulance drove away. It was nearly three o'clock and I dismissed the classes, but added that they could choose to stay if they needed time to settle down or talk to any of the staff about what had happened. Not that we knew what to say. Many did choose to stay as they were too traumatized to get the bus. They weren't the only ones. The only person with any sense of calm was the normally vivacious and loud Keisha; she lay in a total state of relaxation, seemingly oblivious to any of the drama that had just taken place.

"What just happened? I feel so relaxed, I must have fallen asleep. Was it fun?" she asked.

Not exactly.

The tale of this Reiki Day didn't end with the departure of the ambulance. What transpired en route to the hospital was just as disturbing.

According to Denise, inside the ambulance, Suzie had come-to and spoke coherently, as if back in her own rightful body. The Poltergeist voice was gone. Suzie was confused but aware something had happened and that her classmates were concerned about her, but she couldn't remember any more details. She asked Denise to explain exactly what had happened.

"Suzie, I don't think you are ready to hear that yet," Denise replied.

Suzie waited a while before she spoke again.

"She watches over them, you know…your boys. When you take them to school, when you are at home. All the time she is with you and she says to tell you she is very proud of you."

This caused Denise to break down in floods of tears as she thought of her mother's passing the year before. Suzie passed out again leaving a shaken Denise and a very confused attending paramedic who sat there stupefied realizing they were talking to a ghost.

"Can someone please explain what is going on?" he asked.

Denise felt the need to enlighten the poor fellow and carefully explained, "She was in massage class in a Reiki demo which is all about energy, and her body was possessed by an evil spirit. We had to call an ambulance because she was speaking in tongues and foaming at the mouth and…You know what? Never mind."

She also had to explain to the doctor on duty upon arrival at the hospital what had taken place and that no tests would show anything abnormal because it was supernatural. There was no medical explanation. I think the only reason that doctor didn't send her to the psych ward for observation along with Suzie was because Denise proved she was a registered trauma nurse which gave her some—but not much—credibility.

As she sat by Suzie's hospital bed waiting for her to wake up, Denise stood uncharacteristically playing with her hair. It was then that Suzie opened her eyes and said, "Don't be nervous. It's not your mother, it's your grandmother and you know she is present when she strokes your hair like that."

Damage control on campus the next day was a very delicate operation and many of our students remained traumatized. *I remained traumatized!* Upper management and the owners of the school mandated that every student and faculty member attend a presentation by the reiki master herself, who was going to try and make sense of it all.

Ricky stood before the whole school, looking composed as she scanned her wide-eyed audience. The room was full, the air stuffy. No one said a word.

"What we saw yesterday was the power of energy at work. Things like this don't normally happen at my demonstrations," she reassured us. "But yesterday, an evil spirit was unleashed. It had been living inside of Keisha for decades since she was a child. The repercussions of this dormant entity manifested in episodes of intense anger and frustration and pangs in the chest. The energy work unleashed the spirit." She paused and looked around. "But unfortunately, Suzie, who is super sensitive to spirits and was clairvoyant as a young child, let him in. Yes, what you all witnessed yesterday was indeed Suzie being possessed."

And that was the official explanation, the conclusion. After this unexpected and highly unusual lesson on energy massage, there was no doubt in anyone's mind as to its power and the presence of phenomena we cannot see.

The entire experience that December afternoon of 2009 in Philadelphia was disturbing and I still cannot believe what happened. I cannot process or fully understand it even after all these years. It defies all logic. And yes, I do know how crazy it sounds, I really do: bat shit crazy!

Admittedly, if anyone had told *me* this story, I would have said they must be smoking crack, because it is absurd. But it happened. I was there, and I assure you, I wasn't smoking crack. And I swear on my life and on everything that is holy that it is absolutely and completely true.

CHAPTER 13

Hookers and Madams

Churchill: *"Madam, would you sleep with me for five million pounds?"*

Socialite: *"My goodness, Mr. Churchill. Well, I suppose. We would have to discuss terms, of course..."*

Churchill: *"Would you sleep with me for five pounds?"*

Socialite: *"Mr. Churchill, what kind of woman do you think I am?!"*

Churchill: *"Madam, we've already established that. Now we are haggling about the price."*

—Sir Winston Churchill

ANOTHER GRADUATION DAY was fast approaching, and all of the hard work was coming to an end for another class: mastering the complicated anatomy and physiology, the fun and the games, the making fun—not to mention the Poltergeist fiasco. There were celebrations, awards, speeches, proud family and friends in attendance and of course, there were tears.

Graduation days were bittersweet because I hated saying goodbye.

I should have been used to it after two years, but my students became part of my daily life for the nine-month program and I felt a sadness seeing them leave. It was sadness mixed with excitement for them and their futures as massage therapists.

I did my best to keep in touch. There were many great accomplishments and I was proud of each one. I must say, though, that I was more than a little surprised by perhaps the *greatest* accomplishment of my graduates: that of my drowsiest student, Jeff.

To my delight he had landed himself a wonderful job at a busy and popular day spa. He was the most requested therapist and top salesman, making the highest commissions and he even got promoted to lead therapist. When he told me that he was making over $900 a week in his first few months, I was thrilled for him. Who'd have ever thought that the student who slept through the best part of his schooling would go on to do so well?

I wanted him to share his success story and help motivate my new class of students, so I invited him in to do a mini-talk. He wore a suit, gave a speech, answered questions, and I was proud of the professional he had become. He had even shared the wealth and employed two of his classmates.

A few months later I bumped into one of my past graduates who was working for him and we caught up on the latest spa talk.

"Amazing that Jeff finally pulled himself together and made it in the massage world, isn't it?" I remarked.

"Err, actually," she said. "Jeff got fired last week and now he is working back in construction."

"For what?" I gasped.

"For falling asleep on top of clients!"

Yep, on top! I wanted to say, "That would be funny, if it weren't true."

About six months after this meeting, I was sitting in bed late one evening reflecting on another fun, crazy day at school, when I received a phone call from Ed, my fellow instructor. It was a call that broke my heart and made me cry myself to sleep.

"Mandy, I have got something to tell you. It's bad news, I'm afraid. Your old student, Jeff...Sleepy Jeff...he died yesterday."

"What? No! Oh God, no! What the hell happened?"

"Well you know he went back into construction?"

"Yes."

"He fell off a roof. It was a freak accident."

It sounded like one of Jeff's whoppers of a story but tragically this was true, and it was the only time of knowing Jeff that I couldn't laugh at his expense. That news hit me like a punch to the gut; we were both 41 years old.

Shortly after learning of his death I saw his daughter on a cooking show on TV. She was the first kid ever to win the "Chopped" chef championship with her recipe, and she was becoming a huge star. I wished Jeff could have seen her. He would have been a very proud dad, had he not been resting in peace.

Poor Jeff! So, it turned out he wasn't my biggest success story after all; but without a doubt, he was my saddest.

So, who *were* my biggest success stories? That would be Boris and Victoria, two of my graduates from the previous year. But as successful as they were, their accomplishments were not as they appeared to be and begged the questions: *Who are these people? What were they thinking? And who the hell was their teacher?*

As much as we messed around in class, I was serious about keeping the tone professional. I curbed any attempt to joke about happy endings and the like, and God help anyone who tried to degrade or demean the massage industry or associate it with hookers and brothels! I tried so hard to instill this message into all my students, but despite my attempts to keep massage therapy above board, it would seem that not everyone listened.

Boris didn't.

Boris was a good student. He was a tall and muscular Russian with a thick accent and way too much hair. He had a beard and mustache, very hairy legs, hairy arms and a hairy back, but not a strand on his head. He was a good therapist, too. His only problem was his English.

Conversationally, his English was acceptable if you overlooked his accent and his insistence on referring to himself in the third person, but when it came to medical English he suffered. The way in which the test questions were worded was sometimes ambiguous and confusing. If a question was in the negative form such as, "What is NOT a benefit of therapeutic massage?" he couldn't fathom the subtle difference between what was, and was not being asked. I suggested he take extra tutoring after class to help him through.

He and I met regularly on Mondays after class and I gave him practice questions for homework. He focused on each word carefully and jumped out of his chair and cheered when his answer was correct. Face-to-face and with prompts, he understood. He could draw diagrams and show the workings of the heart, so I knew he had grasped the material. But alas, it wasn't enough—the trickery of the national boards exam intimidated him and he failed horribly, guessing at least half of the answers, he confessed.

I felt so bad for him. In those days, failing the boards meant no state license, which in turn meant that employers couldn't legally hire him. In spite of this, Boris said he was going to do his massages from home-to-home for friends and family and see what other opportunities presented themselves while he studied to retake the exam. I applauded him on his perseverance. He graduated the program and we kept in touch. About a year later I received a very disturbing update in the form of an email from him. I can recall what he told me word for word. I replied, and our conversation went like this.

Boris: *About massage business, it make me crazy. Man do not use me much, but woman, yes.*

Me: *But that's good, Boris. There's nothing wrong with having more female clients than males.*

Boris: *Men are very rare to get massage from me. They feel homos.*

But Woman, they get real horny. Is it normal? Boris make more sex than money.

Me: *What do you mean you make more sex than money? What are you saying to these women for them to be getting horny? And where on earth are you doing your massages? This is not what you spent $14,000 on your education for.*

Boris: *What I mean is that during massage they talk about things, you know different things…then they talk about sex…then somehow, we end up having sex. I work from home to home massage. I don't have own place.*

Me: *Boris, that's what hookers do—have sex for money! What are you charging for your…your sexual services?*

Boris: *I charge $45 an hour. Then I get $50-$60 tips. Make double, it's good money.*

Me: *What did I teach you? I taught you to be a professional. You know you shouldn't be crossing the line into prostitution—you know that. What on earth are you thinking?*

Boris: *But I am professional. I am polite, have business card and wear uniform. But I feel destructive. You know?*

Me: *Uhh, YEAH, I do know. That's one thing we can agree on, Boris. It's destructive all right!*

After that conversation, I wanted to destruct him with my own bare hands. I felt betrayed.

I give up! What am I doing this for? What am I trying to prove?

I strived at all times to legitimize my profession, but I was sick to death of constantly having to defend what I did. However did the art of relieving pain through palpation of muscles equate to sex on a table? In class I taught correct draping to ensure client modesty, how to word questions so as not to sound provocative, how to dress so as not to *look* provocative, and how to advertise to create a professional image. All this education ingrained into my students' cerebral cortexes and still, my talented, diligent student felt the need to debase his work?

I was fighting an uphill battle. I was tired of getting angry and offended when people asked jokingly how much my happy endings were. They thought it was a funny comment. It wasn't; it was irksome. I don't know why I took it so personally like it was my job to justify and legitimize my profession to people who didn't get it, who didn't matter.

My loyal clientele, the people who I helped, were the only ones who should have mattered. They knew my worth and the worth of the craft. That said, it didn't change the fact that I, a seasoned expert teaching a new generation of therapists to respect the profession, had clearly failed.

What could I say? I had inadvertently created a male hooker! What a proud teacher I must be! My homegrown gigolo is probably still out there on the streets touting his wares somewhere along the New Jersey Turnpike, and so I implore of you: if you see someone kind of stocky with a bald head wearing blue scrubs who goes by the name of Boris and has a thick Eastern European accent, please slap him for me! Slap him senseless and drop kick him like a football!

Just like Boris, Victoria didn't listen either.

I liked Victoria; she was feisty and sexy and always wore heavy make-up for class, accentuating her full lips with bold red lipstick. She used her looks to work the system to her advantage: a short skirt and a low-cut blouse had secured her the job on more than one occasion. And she was smart; street smart and book smart.

On the street, she carried a knife for protection and in school, she carried her leopard-print tote full of text books and aced most of the tests. In the class on business and marketing, she had demonstrated some entrepreneurial ideas. I had confidence that with this tactical nature and with her ample cleavage, she would go far.

I was right because after graduation I heard that she had indeed become an entrepreneur, had a very successful business and was making a fortune. Ahh, a success story from one of my students to be proud of…Not quite. Not a success story I wanted to put my name to.

Busty Bertha had opened her own business. Good for her! An agency. Also, good. Except that she seemed to have gone off track and become a self-appointed madam running an illegal escort agency under the guise of massage. It was all done by phone from the comfort of her couch with a toddler hanging on to one of her ample assets while she coordinated hook-ups at all times of the day and night.

In any other line of work, I'd have celebrated her fortitude and success, but this made me sad. She had enrolled in school determined to make something of herself and get away from a job in a beauty shop doing massages where she said she was being exploited. It was ironic; it was she who was now doing the exploiting, hiring a cortege of call-girls.

Vic and I had enjoyed a good rapport while she was my student and I thought I had instilled in her the importance of self-worth as well as the opportunities in the growing field of massage therapy. Frustrated and disappointed that my words of wisdom had fallen on her deaf ears and once again feeling like I was wasting my time even trying to legitimize the industry, I called her.

It was late, about 9 p.m. and I was sitting in my living room, going over all my arguments in my head, thinking of the best way to word my questions. I wanted to know everything—well I thought I wanted to know everything, but as it was, I wish I had never asked.

She was happy to hear from me and very matter-of-fact, openly admitting to her madam status. Unfazed by any of it, she defended her career choice saying it was all about power, control and money. This was like a train wreck that I couldn't walk away from.

"What kind of services do you offer?" I asked, running my tired fingers through my short blond hair.

"Anything the client wants, but usually happy endings and that's $100 to $200. We charge more for blow jobs and a lot more for full sex. And if they want the entire night, well that's a grand." She let out a triumphant sigh.

I could picture her sitting in her own row-home living room in Philadelphia where I knew she still lived, her face perfectly made up and smoking a joint.

After a long speechless moment as I processed this information, I asked, "And what is your cut?"

"Fifty percent. It's good money."

"So is robbing banks! Vic, how can you, after graduating massage school and becoming licensed? After all that studying, how can you become a female pimp? How can you cross the line from massage into prostitution?"

"Oh no, I have never done that. I have never crossed the line," she replied.

"What? What do you mean? You sell sex for a living and advertise in the back of newspapers that you're doing massage therapy. That's what we in the business call 'crossing the line.' "

I chewed on my lip as I felt my face flush with anger. My heart-rate quickened as if I was going to throw the first punch. How was the same thing so sacred to me, but nothing more than a means to an end for her? I'd spent nine months wasting my breath. She didn't appear to care and remained blasé, continuing to justify her actions.

"Oh yes, well massage is how we entice them in, but they never *actually* get a massage. That's an hour long and we want them in and out the door. As soon as they have...You know..."

"Yes, yes, I get your point. The question is still, how can you degrade your profession?"

"It is what it is. Massage and sex will always go hand in hand. It's just how it is and always will be."

I refused to believe her nonsense. "No, it isn't. Massage and sex are not inextricably linked. Not in my world. Not ever."

"No, I know it's not the same, but the money is really good and I like the power that comes with it and being in control. I know you're disappointed and don't approve but I'm just being real honest with you. It's not like we allow customers to poop on the girls; we always say no to that request. I mean we do have standards…"

"People *ask* for that? Wait. I don't want to know."

The conversation left me astounded and incredulous that I had been her teacher and had taught her everything she knew. Well, obviously not everything—not how to fend off clients who requested the "masseuse" poop on them! I am happy to say I am not well versed in those kinds of antics.

Didn't she listen to a word I said in class? Apparently not. Was I giving off subliminal messages to my students? Because both Boris and Victoria were two of my highest paid graduates —as a male prostitute and as Philly's youngest madam respectively! This was not part of my master plan.

With these two I had failed as a teacher by epic proportions and my sage advice went unheard. Was it a waste of time trying to make massage therapy something people valued and respected? It was deeply frustrating that even I couldn't make my own students value and respect the craft.

After that disturbing interlude, I became very despondent with my job. It wasn't just Boris and Victoria; the attitudes and apathy of new students were also getting me down. It was 2010 and I had been teaching for nearly two years. Had the novelty worn off? It seemed like the last few months in the classroom offered less banter with the students and more battle. Something had changed. Maybe it was me?

As much as I loved my job, the pay was abysmal and every two weeks when I received my paycheck, my heart sank. It wasn't a salary I could go places with and it was becoming clear there was no room for professional growth within the school. I needed to ask for a raise, or find a better job.

One day I was in a particularly bad mood and it was on the very day that the big shots from corporate were visiting from New York. I was supposed to be on my best behavior when they interviewed all of us, but I was having none of it and instead, I boldly asked for a raise. I pointed out my attributes, qualifications and excellent evaluations. I added that as teachers, we were required to take continuing education units and in the last two years I had become not only national board certified but had also finished up my bachelor's degree.

"I think I am due a raise. I work hard and have been here two years now. So far, any mention of a raise has been met with silence."

Sucking her teeth, one of the partners replied, "Sorry, but there will be no raises for anyone right now."

"So, we are not even worth a couple of dollars an hour increase?" I pushed.

"I am afraid not. We will let you all know if anything changes."

"It's been three years since *any* instructor was given a pay raise. Three *years*! You don't value your staff." I eyed her up and down. "Without us, there would be no school. I am sorry you don't feel we are worth more." Infuriated, I stood and slammed the door on my way out. Amazingly, there were no repercussions from my little outburst, but I wouldn't have even cared if there were.

Apart from the low pay, there were other issues that had started to cloud my love of teaching. Socio-economic issues. It seemed that daily life on the streets of Philadelphia had more challenges than I realized.

One morning I was left completely stumped when one of my students hadn't shown up to class for a couple of weeks and then, suddenly there he was. Lanky and unassuming with tidy dreadlocks, I figured he had been on vacation or was out sick. "Prentice, you haven't been to class in three weeks so you have missed a lot of material. You are going to have to borrow someone's notes and catch up or have private tutoring."

"Yeah, sorry but I was in jail."

My blonde brain blanked. "What? Oh. Right then."

Being banged up did present a problem, of course, but it wasn't the biggest problem we had in the school. The main issue was students smoking dope—coming to school high or smoking it with their classmates on their lunch-break. It seemed that in the City of Brotherly Love, it was normal to smoke pot throughout the day—all the cool kids were doing it—and so I felt the need to address the issue and make my classroom's zero-tolerance policy clear.

Lately, I had been noticing a few pairs of glazed eyes in the classroom. They couldn't possibly be stoned, could they? At first, I thought the students must be tired but then I realized that the glazed look was the result of last night's session or the repercussions of the morning's "wake and bake." So, one morning, instead of proceeding with my original plan to teach the ossification of bones, I found myself having to remind my students that they weren't actually allowed to come into my classroom stoned, high, doped out, spaced out, baked, fried, tripping, or whatever other words they used for being on drugs.

"How are you going to get a job if you have that spaced-out look on your face? Do you think employers are going to go for that? Since when did that constitute professional? Or do you think that your client paying over one hundred dollars for a massage at a spa appreciates the stench of weed coming from their therapist? And it goes without saying that smoking weed every day kills brain cells and there are a few people in this class who don't have many to lose."

My students stared at me as if to say, "Ohhh myyyyy God! You are sooooo old and uncool!"

"Let me just ask you all this," I continued. "Why are you even studying massage therapy if you aren't taking it seriously?"

The twenty-something girl sitting at the front with the lip ring to match her eyebrow ring piped up. "I just want to make $100 an hour like they do at the fancy casinos."

If only she knew.

Her side-kick with glazed eyes put in her two cents. "Yeah, the recruiter who came into our neighborhood told us we can make at least $50 an hour plus tips."

There were high fives and cheers all around.

"And our tuition is free anyway. We don't even have to pay back our student loans. It's a welfare-to-work program," added someone from the back.

So, this was why the majority of the class was in school? I realized that the comments didn't represent everybody, but I sensed an apathy in this new class of students; they were unlike my previous classes. It seemed that half of this class didn't care or have any passion for the field at all; it was just about making a fast buck. *Good luck with that!*

I drove home deflated and dejected. I was so passionate about my work and I had just witnessed complete indifference and aloofness from students who, apparently, only came to school because there was nothing better to do. Shouldn't *they* be the ones with passion? Why didn't they care about their own future as much as I did?

I pondered those questions on my drive home. As I sat in traffic crossing the bridge from Philly into New Jersey, I sipped my daily cappuccino and nibbled on a giant chocolate chip cookie from Starbucks. In rush-hour traffic, I had nothing to do but think. Over-think.

I questioned my own career choice. Just when I thought I was finally happy and settled and making a difference in young people's lives, I felt like I was wasting time lecturing to people who didn't care. And here it was again, the question I had wrestled with the past years: was it time to put my degree to use and get a good, old-fashioned corporate job?

I scribbled on my Starbucks napkin as I sat at the light.

Three reasons for quitting:

1. *Pay was pitiful*

2. *Students weren't hungry for knowledge; they just had the munchies*

3. *I had inadvertently created a hooker and a madam*

Yep, I was ready to move on.

CHAPTER 14

Massaging mammaries for the cure

"No single therapeutic agent can be compared in efficiency with this familiar but perfect tool…the human hand."

—J. Madison Taylor, M.D. 1908

I SAT IN MY small office on the corner of the busy intersection of Church and Church above the chiropractic office, deep in thought about what my next move was going to be. I had continued to rent my small office all the time I was teaching and had kept my regular clientele. For now, they were my bread and butter. But I needed to figure out, was I going to continue to build a clientele full-time like I had done before or embark on something new? I was leaning towards something new. But what?

The phone rang, interrupting my thoughts. It was Mike. I had been massaging Mike and his wife Janine for several years and they had become not only regular clients but good friends. They would both vent to me when they were on the massage table, each complaining about the other when they'd had a squabble, each making me promise not to tell the offending party. It was all done in jest—they were a really cute pair and were always joking around.

So, when Mike called in a cool, deadly serious voice, I knew something was wrong.

"I have to tell you something. I need to get this off my chest," he began.

"What happened? Is everything OK?"

"Well I am not supposed to tell anyone. Janine told me not to, she swore me to secrecy but…"

"Mike, what?"

"JANINE HAS BREAST CANCER!" he blurted out. "We just found out this week. She is beside herself and I don't know what to do to help her."

All I could do was gasp and ask what I thought were the right questions. "What stage is it? What's the prognosis? What's the next step?" I didn't have much experience in dealing with cancer, but I could certainly be a supportive friend.

Mike worked as a teacher at a school for juvenile delinquents. He was in his early forties, balding, with a salt and pepper goatee. He came in for a massage the next day while Janine was still at work, and it did him good to just talk. For once I didn't tell him off for not relaxing and yapping too much. A few days later he convinced his wife to come in, too, as she wasn't sleeping, and she needed to relax.

He made me promise to act normal and pretend I didn't know anything, so as she walked into my office I smiled a big smile and greeted her with, "Hi Janine. How are you today?"

She cocked her head and raised her eyebrows and I knew I had failed miserably in the acting normal department. "OK, you got me. You know that I know, don't you?" I said.

She shrugged. "I figured Mike couldn't keep it from you. He's always been horrible at keeping secrets."

All I could say in response was, "So what are we going to do with you?"

"Just a relaxing aromatherapy with my favorite lavender, please."

I knew how stressed she was but couldn't help but notice how cute she looked. She had an adorable new bob haircut which suited her short, petite frame. Her hair had blonde highlights, unlike last month when she was a redhead. She loved experimenting with new looks and styles.

I massaged the slab of marble that was Janine's back; it was so tight that I tried to get some of the knots out by going deeper where she needed. As I did so, I wondered if maybe I shouldn't be doing this. I honestly didn't know if I was helping her or doing her a disservice. But as she seemed to be enjoying the quiet, falling in and out of sleep, on I plodded. Of course, this was helping! Why wouldn't it be?

I had never worked on anyone with cancer before and as such, I felt desperately unqualified and ill-equipped to help Janine. She didn't seem to notice my shortcomings, but as soon as I got home, I went online and researched massaging people with cancer. I read articles and statistics by experts in the field and learned that less than one percent of massage therapists actually specialize in oncology massage.

That just reinforced the fact that there was a dire need. One article said that with proper training, this work could help people on both a physical and emotional level as they went through surgery, chemotherapy, and convalescence. And even at end of life when care is only of the palliative kind, massage treatments were still beneficial. I wondered why more therapists didn't go into the field. *Was it something I wanted to specialize in?*

I searched for classes in the New Jersey area, but to my frustration, I couldn't find anything. It was already late October, and most courses were over until after the new year. That was almost three months away. Janine needed me immediately and I didn't feel comfortable massaging her again until I knew I was doing it safely. So, I continued to web surf and it wasn't until after midnight that I finally found something.

But it was in Alaska. Alaska, up there next to the North Pole—really far away and practically the other side of the world by my calculations. On top of that, the trip would cost $2,000 with the price of the course and the flight.

Also, it started in mid-November, only three weeks away. That didn't give me much time to get the money together. And what about hotels and food and closing down my business for a week? My teaching salary left me with no disposable cash, so even contemplating the trip seemed pointless. How could I do this? It didn't matter how; I *had* to make this happen. *Come on brain, do your job and think of something!* And then a thought popped into my head—just popped!

I was in the midst of a ten-week spiritual growth class called *Prosperity Plus* held on Monday nights at our cool church, Joyful Gathering. It was taught by our equally cool reverend, Reverend Margaret. She was from England, like me, and she taught us about the Laws of the Universe, specifically The Law of Attraction, and how we are the creators of our own destiny. In one of the lessons, we were learning how to manifest what we wanted by focusing on it, journaling it and believing it.

What if I did this for the class in Alaska? Focusing should be easy. Better do a bit of meditation and imagine Alaska.

Sitting down with my eyes closed, I envisioned snow and mountains, ten-foot grizzly bears, polar bears on ice, and me wearing warm, fat fluffy boots to class. I meditated on these images for a moment and then wrote it all down. Just then, another thought popped into my head right next to the first one: what if my friends would sponsor me to go? All I had to do was ask—*ask and it is given.*

If 20 people thought it important enough for me to study oncology massage and if they would consider "sponsoring" me—well, essentially donating a hundred bucks—then I would be able to go. It was a bit cheeky but what did I have to lose? It was for the greater good, right? With that in mind, I put it out there into the Universe.

Putting it out there to the Universe was tantamount to putting it on social media. The response I received from my Facebook friends was immediate, if not overwhelming. People tossed money at me like I was a stripper dancing on a pole!

Even strangers pledged money. In three days I raised just over my $2,000 target. I had all the money I needed for a plane ticket, a hotel room, and a new white poofy coat, because everybody knows it is minus a million degrees up there at the North Pole. And just like that, my Alaska trip had manifested: it certainly was *Prosperity Plus!*

It was three weeks until my trip and in that time, it seemed that cancer was all around me. It was even on my answering machine in the form of a distressing voicemail from Ingrid—Frenchie—my old reflexology client who had come to me years before, looking to cure her chronic constipation. She had been diagnosed with breast cancer five years prior but had been in remission and was thriving.

The last time I saw her was three months before and we walked in the woods—just the two of us. She was in good spirits talking about her post-mastectomy reconstruction, joking about how her right boob was hairy because the doctors had taken a skin graft from her pubic area. We had a good laugh about it.

Now, as I listened to her message, my heart sank as I heard her frail voice telling me the cancer had come back with a vengeance. This time it was an aggressive strain and had metastasized to her bones. She was in hospital after another surgery and undergoing more chemotherapy.

We spoke only one more time over the next few days and then her phone calls stopped coming. I kept the last message from her and listened to it over and over just to hear her cute little French accent.

Five days later, I listened to another message from her husband. It was the one I had been expecting but didn't want to hear, the one that said Ingrid had died in the night. We were born one day apart. And we were only 41.

Two days before I was due to fly to Alaska, I found myself at Ingrid's funeral. In accordance with her Buddhist faith, the service was four days after her death and it was as beautiful and classy as she was. It was held on a snowy day at the monastery she used to go to outside of Washington D.C. and it was her wish for her ashes to be scattered by her friends around the stone water fountain in the rose garden. I didn't know if I could; it was too real and I stood motionless as her husband offered me the box of ashes. It was ironic; I was holding the remains of the body that I used to massage—the same body that was now dust on my fingers. I stood and wept, scattering Ingrid, whose feet always smelled of roses, in the rose garden.

Two days later, still mourning the loss of my friend to cancer, I boarded my plane to go and study oncology massage. More than ever, I felt my decision to go into the field was the right one.

Clad in extremely ugly, passion-killing thermal underwear, I arrived up north in the land of the grizzly bear. I had ridden camels in the middle of the desert in Egypt, trekked through the jungle with the hill tribes in Thailand, but Alaska, which is officially part of the U.S, was indeed a culture shock. I wasn't expecting to see Eskimos, reindeer sausages on menus, lunatics climbing icicles, or moose holding up traffic in the middle of the highway. And that was on my first day!

That first day, I had a free morning in Anchorage before I had to make the drive further south to the class in Homer, so I planned to venture by bus into the capital for a nice, hearty breakfast. But it was still pitch-black outside and I felt safer waiting in my hotel until daylight. I waited...and I waited.

To pass the time until sunrise I made coffee and watched the news. I opened the curtains, but still no daylight. I made more coffee and looked out the window again. Outside it remained black as the Ace of Spades and it was now past 9 a.m. I called down to reception.

"Good morning. I don't mean to state the obvious, but it's nine o'clock in the morning and it's still pitch-black outside. Are we expecting daylight any time soon?"

It was a bit of a funny question really, but I was physically and figuratively in the dark. The woman at the end of the line informed me that the daylight wouldn't be making its appearance for at least another half an hour. I didn't have much time so with no other choice, I checked out of the hotel and stepped out into what looked like the middle of the night, and waited with the locals to catch the bus.

On the ride into town, I took out my articles on oncology massage and began to read up. The mainstream massage textbooks shy away from working on clients with cancer for fear that any stimulation could potentially cause its spread. It's a fair assumption, but according to what I was reading, this was erroneous thinking and unsubstantiated. I was fascinated by one article I had printed out. Authors Cheryl Chapman and Eileen Kennedy wrote, *"Cancer can spread with little or no activity such as sleeping, breathing, eating, walking, etc. Therefore, there is every reason to believe that gentle, light or compassionate touch can be administered safely and effectively, provided that no direct pressure or massage is applied to the traumatized area affected by the disease."*

That sounded perfectly reasonable to me. I wanted to continue reading but I'd come to my stop, so I stepped off the bus. It was now past 10 a.m. and I was starving. I had to walk four blocks to the breakfast café.

God, it was cold! *Did I get off at the wrong stop and end up on Neptune?* I had never felt that freezing cold before in my life. I couldn't even feel my face or my lips enough to enunciate, "Table for one please."

I sat down and hoped I would thaw out before the waitress came, and as I set myself to defrost, I pulled out some more reading material. It was in the form of a cute little book on healthy breast massage entitled, *The Happy Breast Book* written by Cheryl Chapman, whose article I had just read. The book lifted the taboo, making it not only acceptable, but smart, for women to massage their own mammaries. What did she call it? "Phluffing the girls!" This meant wiggling and jiggling them by pulling our bra straps up and down making them bounce, and leaning over to shake them, tap them, lift them and side-swipe them. She believed this boob aerobics kept the breast tissue healthy by increasing the blood circulation and draining out toxins. The philosophy made complete sense.

I thought about the last time my own boobs had been massaged. It was at the hammam at the Parisian mosque. I wondered if my rotund Arabic masseuse realized just how much she was benefitting her clients, or how scientific her wax on, wax off moves were.

I looked around the café and noticed that the locals were wearing those big long furry coats with fur hoods around their faces and my only frame of reference for this was Eskimo. I sat staring in awe as it seemed that everyone in the café was dressed like the characters I remembered from my childhood storybooks! I wondered why they were staring back at me.

Oh, they are staring at my book with a picture of big boobs on the front.

I chuckled to myself, put my book away and read the menu instead.

I gasped: reindeer sausage and eggs? Reindeer patty melt? There was also reindeer scramble with peppers and a hearty reindeer stew. I really was experiencing culture shock. People really ate reindeer?

"Are you ready to order?" the waitress asked.

"Just pancakes, please."

I couldn't stomach Rudolf for breakfast.

It seemed that my lessons in culture were to continue for the remainder of the day. During the four-hour drive along the coast to Homer I was shocked to see groups of Alaskans, obviously with a death wish, rock-climbing up icicles on a cliff at the side of Seward Highway, using ice picks! Who in their right mind climbs icicles right next to ongoing traffic? And how were their eyeballs not freezing over in those sub-zero temperatures?

Suddenly, traffic came to a halt and I wondered what was causing the hold-up. It was a moose. It was a very ugly, over-sized moose with big antlers standing stubbornly in the middle of the two-lane highway, apparently refusing to budge. Imagine a moose stopping traffic on the New Jersey Turnpike! Said moose finally decided to go home and I went on my merry way driving past the icicle climbers to the left and the shore to the right. When I saw the waves had frozen over mid curl and the entire bay had become a giant natural ice-rink, I realized just how cold it was.

It was past 4 p.m. and already dark, but the local kids were still outside playing on the ice. They were racing each other and doing pirouettes for fun—not on skates but in their cars. Although this looked like party central with headlights like laser beams dancing in all directions, it also looked rather dangerous. Was this even legal? There were no police in sight to reprimand them or issue them tickets—they weren't dumb. It was too cold to be outside; the cops were probably taking a break in warm cafes and eating reindeer pies!

Arriving at the seaside resort of Homer, I was eager to settle in to my hotel room and warm up. I was staying at a little wooden inn on a gray sandy beach which wrapped around the far end of the peninsula. It was touted as being "at the edge of the world" and looking at it on a world map, it certainly was.

My room had an almost floor-to-ceiling window overlooking stunning mountainous peeks and the frozen sea. The beach, like everything else in Alaska in November, was covered in clean white snow, and dotted with pieces of driftwood. It was beautiful in the dark because the moon and the stars lit it all up making every-thing glisten. I was sitting in the middle of a Christmas card—all I needed was Santa and some eggnog. This breathtaking winter wonderland was to be my home for the next week and the back-drop for my class, starting early the next day.

Before I settled in for the night, I read some more. I was excited and nervous at the same time about pursuing oncology massage, but I had a feeling that this week of study in Alaska was going to be a turning point in my career. If I was cut out for it.

The following morning, wrapped up in my thermal underwear, padded white knee-length coat, insulated gloves and white snow boots that looked too big for me, I drove to the class looking like the Michelin Man.

I was excited to meet the teacher, a native Alaskan called Jane, one of the leading experts in the field of oncology massage specializing in working with post-surgery clients. When I arrived at the venue, a private home located in town, Jane stood tall with mousy-blonde short hair, welcoming us inside—me and six other therapists from all over the country. She exuded a calming presence, which I thought was perfect for teaching the serious topic of cancer.

Our first lesson wasn't dissimilar from any other massage therapy class. Jane began with theory—essentially an anatomy and physiology review with a focus primarily on the lymphatic system, our toxic drainage system. This made sense because it's our body's human plumbing system, and the one most affected by cancer treatments like mastectomy, lymph node removal, chemo and radiation. I was astonished to learn how important these lymph nodes were. They were essentially drains and if even one of them was removed, strict protocol had to be followed, otherwise massage could do more damage than good.

"What happens if a client neglects to inform us of a lymph node removal?" I asked.

"That's why thorough questionnaires are essential," Jane nodded thoughtfully. "Massaging a compromised system can result in severe, painful swelling of the arms and it's not uncommon for arms to triple in size—a debilitating condition called lymphedema. Once a person has it, they have it for life. It can only be managed."

That seemed a bit unfair to me.

It soon became obvious that oncology massage was more about what *not* to do than how to actually administer the massage itself. Imagine if untrained or inexperienced graduates tried to work on clients whose nodes had been removed. They might automatically think to do Swedish strokes to increase circulation, or give a deep tissue to work out tight shoulders, not realizing they could inadvertently cause lymphedema and ruin someone's life. Literally.

On the flip side of that coin, it truly surprised me just how much an oncology massage *could* help. Light lymphatic drainage techniques help detox the body and reduce swelling, and the very nature of touch stimulates the nerve endings in the skin, helping to restore feeling.

But perhaps the biggest claim of oncology massage is that it helps reduce anxiety and depression, especially pre-surgery anxiety. Knowing how beneficial it could be, it annoyed me immensely that the general consensus was not to treat people going through cancer. They were the ones who needed it the most! So many schools, spas and even licensed therapists were of this school of thought. I decided it was my duty to help change that.

I was enjoying the class. I liked that it wasn't just theory. Apart from the philosophy, we learned about how music positively affects the treatment, too. If the same music from a client's massage sessions is played during the actual surgery, it provides a level of comfort and familiarity and reduces anxiety—especially if the music contains subliminal healing messages. I had never thought of that.

To my surprise, we were also taught how to use different language to be diplomatic and use more tact and sensitivity. My peers had some good questions about how to broach certain situations and not say the wrong thing.

"What happens if you need to massage the client's head but they have a wig on? What's the polite terminology? And how do you ask about a weird blotch on the skin without being rude?" asked one of the local students from Anchorage.

Our teacher replied, "Well, the question 'Are you wearing a

wig?' becomes 'How would you like me to work with your head?' and if there are strange skin conditions you have never seen before, rather than risking insult, just ask 'Is your doctor concerned about these bruises, blotches, discolorations?' "

Of course, the language had to be different, yet it had never occurred to me until my fellow student mentioned it. I knew I had a lot of work to do on the art of subtlety, so I wrote all the advice down, word for word.

"What about if the client insists on something which you know is against protocol? Like if they want deep massage on the legs?" I asked.

"Use specific verbiage along the lines of, 'Given your history there is blood clot risk in the legs, but we can focus on the upper body.'"

She was good! Yes, it was all about proper bedside manners.

On the third day we had practical clinic where we put our new skills to the test and worked on local volunteers who either had cancer or were post-mastectomy. Our volunteers were in their twenties, thirties, seventies; they were moms, grandmothers, someone's daughter and someone's best friend. Those brave women whipped off their tops for the greater good with no prudishness or shame, revealing their scars and cut-up torsos for us to study. Some women had chosen double mastectomy with reconstruction so there was no sign of the surgery—just beautifully done breast implants. Others had chosen to forgo reconstruction and lived with scars where their breasts had once been. They graciously allowed us to massage those scars.

For scar work, we used neem oil, an Indian antiseptic oil which smells of peanut and garlic, and helped reduce the appearance of the lesion. We also sent our clients home with oil so they could continue with self-massage, encouraging them to touch their incisions and reconnect with their bodies. This was a very important step in the healing process.

Seeing cancer in the raw was both shocking and frightening at the same time, and hearing some of the personal stories wrenched my heart. I had to be brave and not get too emotional. After all, my job was to create a space for *their* healing, not to stand there and blub like a child at the unfairness of it all.

Every day class ended at 4 p.m. and we students went back to our respective hotels—in the dark. Class was so intense I hardly saw the sunlight because we started in the dark at 9 a.m. and by the end of class, the daylight had already been and gone, and it was pitch black again. Having seen daylight in Alaska for about a minute and a half the entire week, I headed back home to New Jersey to put my new knowledge to use and massage my friend and client, Janine, post-mastectomy. I was quite proud of my new certification.

While I enjoyed learning the new modality of oncology massage, I still had more to absorb. It was pretty heavy and could be emotionally draining at times, so I was happy I still had my *Prosperity Plus* classes at church to take my mind off it a bit.

I was even happier I had tickets to an upcoming Olivia Newton-John concert to look forward to in a few days. Little did I know then she would be such an inspiration in my massage career...

CHAPTER 15

Inspired by Olivia Newton-John

"To me luxury is to be at home with my daughter, and the occasional massage doesn't hurt."

—Olivia Newton-John.

ONDAY NIGHT'S CLASS INCLUDED filling out a worksheet entitled, *"Five Things I Want to Do before I Die."* Meeting Olivia was number three on my list. As I wrote the words, I wondered if it was even possible; she was such a big star. But since the whole point of this class was to teach that absolutely anything *is* possible, I stopped wondering and decided to believe wholeheartedly that it was. And besides, my Alaska trip was proof positive that the Law of Attraction works: what you focus on expands.

My idea of focusing was putting on her greatest hits album and I went to her website to see what was new. I didn't know she did "meet and greets" backstage to raise funds for her cancer center? Could I really meet her with just one click?

Click, donate, print receipt.

It turned out that I could, and suddenly my childhood dream was about to come true the very next evening.

I knew I wouldn't be able to sleep that night, so I lay on the couch watching Olivia and Deepak Chopra in the *Seven Spiritual Laws of Success* documentary which featured Olivia's new healing music from her *Grace and Gratitude* album. I must have dozed off around 3 a.m. The last thing I remembered was hearing the words to *Learn to Love Yourself*.

I drifted in and out of sleep, half dreaming, and I felt she was really with me. Right there. Like an angel. So surreal...so weird. Clearly, I must still be jet-lagged from Alaska!

The following night after an amazing show of old songs, new songs, country songs and songs from Grease, I stood in line with my VIP backstage pass. Me, VIP! I had bought a new black mini-dress with see-through sleeves and silver sequins and studs on the collar and cuffs, and I felt fabulous! I waited by the stage, bouncing at the knees in excitement, with the other die-hard fans until finally it was my turn.

And then, there I was in my early forties face-to-face with someone I had idolized since I was an eight-year-old girl. I felt like a child almost hyperventilating. Olivia Newton-John looked even more beautiful in real life with a huge welcoming red-lipped smile. I threw my arms around her in gratitude. Isn't that how you're supposed to greet your idol?

"Hi Olivia. I have loved you since I was eight." I smiled so hard my cheeks burned.

"Oh, you're English?" she asked. "What's your name?"

I took a deep breath. I must have spoken a mile a minute trying to get in all 35 years of what I wanted to say because I knew I wouldn't have much time with her. She must have thought I had verbal diarrhea.

I had also written her a letter which I gave to her along with a beautiful photo of her to sign. She asked where the photo was taken and I told her it was from *The Seven Spiritual Laws of Success*. I added that I too believed in synchronicity and, as such, had manifested this meeting with her. I even showed her that she was number three on my *Five Things I Want to Do Before I Die* list, which made her smile. She didn't look at me for even one second like I was a nut job.

"Olivia, I wanted to tell you I am a massage therapist and I play your healing music as I work, and also that I just got back from Alaska from a post-mastectomy massage class. One of my clients has breast cancer and I wanted to help her."

"That's wonderful!" she beamed. "We do that too in my spa in Australia."

"Yes, I know. I would love to go to Gaia one day."

We had a lot to talk about, she as a spokeswoman for cancer survivors—being one herself—and I, with my new passion for working with cancer patients. I think we could have talked all day on the subject, but sadly I had to let her go to meet and greet her other fans. We had some photos taken together, I hugged her again and reluctantly said goodbye. I was so emotional and overwhelmed, tears of happiness streamed down my face as I exited the concert hall.

After talking to Olivia, I felt even more inspired to further my studies. I added another thing I wanted to do before I die—go to Gaia. I put it on my list and did my best to quash all thoughts of venturing Down Under for then, and focus on taking some more training.

A few weeks later, on a cold February morning, I set off on a six-hour road-trip to Boston to study with another prominent figure in the field of oncology massage. I'd taken her online classes and was eager to take her hands-on course.

The class was held in a large massage center which felt like a yoga studio—very peaceful with good energy. About 40 students showed up for the week-long seminar. The room was packed.

The theory classes in Boston were similar to those I had taken in Alaska, so that part was a refresher class for me. We also went into great detail about taking precautions with our lymphedema clients, but some precautions seemed a bit over the top. Was it really necessary to disinfect door knobs and take plants and trickling water fountains out of the office? Apparently, it was. If white blood cells are low—a condition called *neutropenia*—people are much more susceptible to infection and in extreme cases, disinfecting is imperative because of the risk of microbes. Whoever would have thought I'd have to worry about microbes on my doorknobs!

The training made me realize how careful I needed to be. In fact, I learned the massage I had been doing with lavender essential oil on Janine was, in fact, *not* a smart thing to do because lavender is an estrogen enhancer and cancer feeds off estrogen! How was I to know that I had been doing it all wrong? Aghhh…epic fail!

I should have used something like sandalwood which acts as an antiseptic and sedative, and is good for depression and scars and nerve sensitivity. Or ginger and spearmint which are good for post-chemotherapy nausea. I was learning that not all essential oils are created equal.

On the third day of class we delved into mastering a few magic tricks in the practical class.

The first was a subtle trick. It was the art of simply cradling the head in our hands, and it worked like magic. All we therapists were doing was sitting at the top of the table holding our clients' heads in our hands as if holding a large watermelon. It looked like we weren't doing anything at all, but by simply holding, we were creating a healing space giving the client permission to just be, and a sense of absolute nurturing.

As we practiced on each other, many therapists broke down in tears including me; the holding triggered such an emotional release. I didn't expect to be choked-up or blubbing during my training but there was such a sense of being cared for, of unconditional love. Laying on the table with someone embracing me made me feel secure, safe and empowered. I imagined it must be even more empowering for people going through cancer.

My favorite magic trick was making the client float on air—yes, float! Not in the magic show sense of the word, but creative bolstering and pillow support produced a feeling of weightlessness as there was no pressure anywhere on the body. We rolled up towels of various sizes and placed them under the ankles, wrists, neck, small of the back, knees, hips, and shoulders. It was quite a production in that it took a good ten minutes or more to do, but it was well worth it.

The client was totally supported and cradled, which is the intention of palliative care, and even though it took very little effort on our part, simply rolling up some old towels, it was the essence of luxury and pampering. Being bolstered and feeling like you were floating made it very easy to drift off to sleep. Sleep was one of the main goals for clients experiencing insomnia and anxiety because when the body is sleeping, it instinctively knows how to heal itself. I loved this trick; the client became Aladdin and the table turned into a magic carpet.

My classes were eye-opening and I learned more than I expected. It wasn't just the physiology or the massage strokes; compassion and empathy were part and parcel of dealing with cancer and all its emotional trimmings. My quest to rub people was once again leading to a much deeper meaning. A very different offshoot of massage therapy certainly gave me purpose.

Back in my office in New Jersey armed with my pink binders full of information from all my classes, I decided I was all in and I was going to re-invent my practice and be the one percent of therapists in the U.S who specialized in oncology massage.

I redecorated, re-carpeted, and repainted in my favorite aqua blue that reminded me of the Caribbean Sea and Tiffany's. Soon, I created two new absolutely beautiful soothing healing rooms which were dimly lit and a pleasure to work in. I renamed my business, too: Grace and Gratitude Cancer Massage Center after Olivia Newton-John's healing album. I was ready to go.

By then, Janine had already had her mastectomy and was recovering nicely. She still felt weak however, and she didn't like how her new implants felt.

"They are like over-inflated footballs," she told me one sunny day as I stood in her suburban home in South Jersey. "They are so big I can barely see my feet!"

"What do you want to see your feet for?" I rubbed her shoulder in consolation. "They will settle in. Give them a few more weeks."

"Feel them! Go on, squeeze them," she said, pulling her hot pink *Fuck Cancer* t-shirt over her head.

So, I did as I was told and squeezed them. They were too big for my outspread hands. "Yep. Over-inflated footballs!" We both laughed.

I visited Janine regularly at her home and thanks to my classes, I felt better equipped to be massaging her. I had no self-doubt or fear and with my newly acquired bedside manner, when she asked for her favorite lavender oil, I said "Janine, given your estrogen levels, lavender wouldn't be the best option. But I do have some lovely sandalwood." I had been paying attention in the class on bedside manners!

I began to see new clients, as well as people who had heard I was offering free massages as part of my grand re-opening for anyone going through cancer—anyone who was receiving chemotherapy, radiation or who was post-surgery. I incorporated the protocols I had learned in Alaska and Boston and I removed the plants from my office, put away my lavender oil, and even wiped my doorknobs down.

The only issue I had with my new specialty was that I found it impossible to hold back my tears, especially when the people in front of me were in the biggest fight of their lives, opening their hearts and sharing such raw emotion. My clients' honesty was both the blessing and the curse of being a therapist: people shared their emotions, their fears, and their deepest darkest secrets.

Over the next six months, I saw people with lung cancer, women with breast cancer, and men with breast cancer. It seems almost counterintuitive to say that I saw *men* with breast cancer but, although it is not as common as it is in women, men absolutely do get it. And it's not called chest cancer either, as one might think; it is still called breast cancer. Was this common knowledge? I didn't know any of this until I became a massage therapist.

It also seemed counterintuitive to see people with lung cancer who have never smoked a cigarette in their entire lives. This was the case with Will. Will came to me with stage 4 lung cancer, which was desperately unfair considering he had never taken a puff in his 24 years. At stage 4, the prognosis was dismal at best, and it was for the most part, a waiting game. Did he have months? Weeks?

He showed up in my office for the first time in late March, thirty pounds under his normal weight. A few strands of mis-placed blond hair remained on his head after the chemo. He shiv-ered as he lay on my warm massage table and talked to me about his young wife and three-year-old little boy.

Will had everything to live for. It was heartbreaking to see him so weak and in pain with so many questions unanswered. I made him comfortable and covered his eyes, doing the luxury bolstering massages so he could float for an hour pain-free. I covered his eyes not only for his comfort but also to hide my own tears. It was hard to pull myself together and, without him noticing, I sniveled throughout the entire session at the cruelty of it all.

Unlike Will, on the flip side of the cigarette coin, were people who had smoked all of their lives and they too were facing the same dismal prognosis. Not only were they dealing with the dis-ease, they were also dealing with self-blame, self-hatred, intense shame for what they, themselves, felt was self-inflicted. This was how Claire felt.

Claire had smoked for over 20 years. Her lung cancer was stage two. She shared her story of how she went to a PTA meeting at her daughter's elementary school soon after her diagnosis. When she told the other parents her news, the first question anyone asked, and the PTA moms were no exception, was if she smoked. When she admitted that she had, shame consumed her and, although no one ever voiced the words, their expressions clearly said, "What on earth did you expect?"

This judgment, she confided, was all it took to make her feel even guiltier and take on another mountain of self-hatred. As she relayed her experience, she looked into my eyes as if searching for some kind of validation. I held her hand, nodded and let her continue. My new bedside manners told me that sometimes I didn't need to say anything; sometimes people just needed to be heard.

In my new role as an oncology massage therapist, I had to ask myself if I'd taken on too much. I was pondering this question when Maryanne walked into my office.

Maryanne worked as a school teacher, and had been diagnosed with stage 1 breast cancer. Erring on the side of caution, she'd recently had a double mastectomy. They'd cut her up pretty badly, and the surgery left her heavily scarred.

She asked me if I could do just one thing.

"I need you to soften the tough scars and the whole area around my breasts because if the breast tissue isn't pliable enough, my doctor said she won't be able to put the implants in. Can you do it?"

That might have been a tall order but with no lymph node removal, luck was on our side. There was no threat of lymphedema. This meant I could massage more vigorously than protocol usually allowed, and I could stretch and soften the scars.

Maryanne and I had about six weeks to meet our goal, and twice a week I massaged the area where her breasts had been lopped off. The deep tissue strokes and scar tissue work were painful for her at times but she didn't complain; she just wanted the treatments to work. And they did.

I gave her homework to do and between the pair of us we prepared her body for a new pair of breasts—breasts that were perfect and cancer-free. Her surgeon was absolutely amazed at how supple the scar tissue was, and this paved the way for a successful surgery. I am proud to say that I was able to help Maryanne. And Claire.

But it was too late for Will.

I had a long way to go to build my practice but I was content in my work. It was work worthy of respect and in some cases, life-changing for my clients. I was proud to be not only a massage therapist, but one who now specialized in oncology massage. I had big plans for this new venture.

Taking a break for my birthday, I boarded a train up to New York City for a book signing. It wasn't just any book signing; Olivia Newton-John had written a new cookbook for health called *LiveWise*. I was going to see her again!

I waited in a long line of at least three or four hundred people in Barnes and Noble as my loving and patient husband sat in the pub next door, drinking Guinness and coming in and out to bring me coffees and snacks throughout the day.

After waiting over three hours in line with other fans, many of whom I had met at the concert and meet-and-greet the year before, it was finally my turn. Olivia sat at her book table wearing a cream Chanel suit. Her hair rested shoulder-length, light blonde and straightened. She smiled her usual cheeky smile as she indulged in playful banter with the photographers.

I nearly burst when she nodded at me in recognition.

"Do you remember I told you I was studying oncology massage in Alaska? Well, I am now specializing in it and opened a small center. It's called Grace and Gratitude Cancer Massage Center," I said proudly.

I showed her photos of my two gorgeous Tiffany-blue rooms. She couldn't stop looking at them, saying how beautiful they were.

"You named your oncology massage practice after my song?" she tilted her head with a proud smile.

"Yes, you were my inspiration," I beamed.

I gave her my new business card and we had another photo taken together, which is my favorite so far. I framed it and hung it in my office.

A month later, to my utter delight, I received a hand-written letter from her saying how thrilled she was with what I was doing.

She wished me luck and asked if I would keep in touch and keep her informed of how it was all going. Which I did.

It was all confirmation I was on the right path. I was once again fulfilled in my career choice and content in my decision to remain in the field.

If this wasn't a real job, then I don't know what is!

I had reignited the flame in my massage career—a flame which I thought had gone out after giving up teaching. But once again my work felt more valuable than ever. Never for a moment did I think I would be doing palliative care or end-of-life massage. I was honored and had a good feeling about the future. I was going to go far.

And I did go far. But it was not in the direction I had planned at all.

With one phone call, my dreams were shattered.

Only a few months later, at the beginning of summer my husband called with news that crushed me. The military was sending us to Spain. A new assignment. We had to be there in twelve weeks. That was just 84 days away!

Sitting in my living room when I received the call, I slumped in a sobbing heap on the floor. "No! I can't. I have my work!"

"Mandy, we don't have a choice. I was given orders. Unless you don't want to go with me."

I wailed uncontrollably and inconsolably. "I've worked hard for this new business," I sobbed. "I've traveled so far to get certified and have poured my heart and soul into it. What about my clients? They need me."

I felt numb. Panic-stricken. What was I going to do with my business? How could I keep it going? I didn't want it to die.

For days, I sat sobbing, incredulous and devoid of feeling, not willing to accept the painful truth that I couldn't afford to keep Grace and Gratitude going or run it from nearly four thousand miles away. I had to leave it all behind. I couldn't sell the business either, although I tried, because oncology massage was too specialized and there were very few people in New Jersey who were certified.

For weeks, I stewed. I could barely even look at my husband, although I knew my anger was misdirected and the transfer wasn't his fault. I could have stayed but we had a really happy marriage and I wanted to be with him. In rivers of tears, trying to swim upstream and with a sense of total defeat, I wailed in Reverend Margaret's arms at the cruel turn of events. She took it in stride and said, "You have shown that you can create something beautiful and you can do that again. Here, Spain, anywhere."

Even though her words comforted me, and I knew I had skills that no one could take away, I remained inconsolable.

For months, I mourned the loss of my beautiful Tiffany-blue oncology massage center. How could massage be more useful than this?

CHAPTER 16

Masseuse to the troops in Spain

"Bob Hope got a massage every day of his life for 63 years and lived to be 100. A coincidence? I think not."

—Mandy Urena

ANY NORMAL PERSON faced with the prospect of moving to sunny southern Spain would have been elated. But I went kicking and screaming. Indeed, I put up a fuss for a good few months, but then, as much as I refused to admit it, the small naval base in Rota to which we had been assigned was exactly where I needed to be.

It was ironic, but in the space of a year, my clientele had changed from people who were fighting disease, to lean, mean fighting machines at the peak of their fitness. I had inadvertently become the masseuse to the troops.

I was very fortunate in that as soon as I arrived in that wonderfully charming small-town, I landed a massage gig at the base gym working weekdays while another Spanish therapist worked weekends. Naval Station Rota was a joint navy base with a very small air force contingency, a marine company and a smattering of soldiers in the army, so my new clientele was made up of military personnel representing all of our American armed forces on land, air and sea. It was the second time I had landed myself a job at the base gym, my first being in Germany, so I was used to massaging the military.

I wasn't however, used to massaging the special forces that were EOD.

EOD served the navy's Explosive Ordnance Disposal Squad—the bomb squad, as we would call them in England. They were in a league of their own and, being special forces, were hailed as the fittest and finest members of the navy. Everyone could see they were fit and fine because they ran around the base flaunting their shirtless, tanned bodies in only the very tiniest of government-issued gym shorts. These sightings were a daily occurrence and a truck load of these half-naked troops in the back of a pick-up was part of the landscape. Had I not known better, I'd have thought they were promoting an upcoming all-male revue. I couldn't help but stand mouth open, like a lizard catching flies. Yes, I liked my new work environment. And I'd be lying if I said I didn't fully appreciate the opportunity to massage a beautiful latissimus dorsi and a lovely gluteus maximus once in a while. And besides, those body-builders needed deep tissue massages, myofascial release massages, and pre-or post-workout sports massages to keep them healthy and ready for battle. It was my duty to take care of those buff Adonises, and it was my job to help remove lactic acid which had built up in their carefully sculpted, lovingly pumped muscle fibers. Even though I am a professional, I am neither blind nor dead, so when I see beautiful muscles on my table I must admit I think to myself, I do love my job!

But special forces like EOD were hard work. They were always jumping out of planes, detonating bombs and injuring themselves, and they would come to me in desperation when something was busted up.

It was usually lower back, hip or groin injuries from intense training, and fixing them up required working on their glutes, lateral hip rotators and ileo-psoas, and these were all muscles located on the butt and the inner thigh. Working out the knots in these muscles could sometimes be a very delicate operation and not a task for the bashful or the faint of heart.

When those elite soldiers booked an appointment, I knew I was going to have to get up close and personal and that the client needed to be open and comfortable with a) the pain and b) a complete stranger being barely an inch away from their unmentionables. It also required Herculean strength on my part, lifting and stretching these buff and heavy machines; their legs alone weighed a ton!

It seemed that I was doing the same moves on all the EOD guys as they all showed up with the same injuries. I would start with them lying face down so I could warm up the hamstrings, the I.T. band on the sides of the legs and the large glute muscles. Then I would bend the knee out to the side like a frog so I could access the otherwise inaccessible undercarriage, and in that position, I would knead and squeeze and prod the offending muscles and sink my elbow in deep using all the pressure I could muster. It required some very careful draping, too, so that things didn't fall out.

This wasn't the kind of massage where the client could nod off; it was sports massage and they had to participate in the PNF stretching. PNF stood for proprioceptive neuromuscular facilitation—a mouthful to say but which simply meant active-resisted stretching to maximize flexibility. I push, they resist and then when they relax, I push again for a deeper stretch. It was gymnastics for me climbing up on the table and twisting their bodies into a pretzel, raising their legs over their heads, and it took all the muscle strength I had. It was ironic; after fixing up Popeye-the-Sailor, I felt so worn out I needed a bit of TLC myself—and maybe a bit of spinach, too!

It wasn't a sacrifice though. I felt privileged to be helping these guys who retrieved bodies from the bottom of the ocean or risked their lives defusing bombs in airports and shopping malls. Someone needed to take care of them.

I loved massaging the military and there was never a dull

moment; when I wasn't busy maneuvering ungracefully around groins, I was massaging drunken sailors!

When a fleet of navy ships came in from long deployments every few months, mayhem ensued. Sailors were unleashed in Rota for some long-awaited R and R. I imagined the young seamen cramped in their bunks for months on end. Who needed a massage more than they did?

I suggested to management at the gym that we offer chair massage down at the docks to welcome them, but they pointed out that it would be too dangerous with so much machinery around. They proposed that the club with its bar, restaurant, Wi-Fi hook-ups, and mini gaming room, would be a safer venue. For the sailors' first night in town, the base organized a huge party with a DJ to welcome them to port.

The idea was to start early before the imbibing began.

At four in the afternoon, I arrived at the club dressed in my bright red scrubs and a pair of comfortable sneakers. My Spanish counterpart arrived soon afterwards and we began to set up. The two of us would be giving seated chair massages similar to the ones in busy shopping malls, where the clients sit leaning forward with their head in a cushioned face hole and their feet hooked over a padded foot rest. In this position, they are fully supported and it feels like being suspended in air; it's really quite comfortable and there is no need to remove any clothing so it's easy for people to jump on and off.

We put a little sign up saying "Chair Massage, $1 a minute," and set up our chairs and waited. Two hours later, right around six p.m. the sailors were finally dismissed and started trickling in. My Spanish colleague decided the event was going to be a dud and made up some excuse about her babysitter being sick and left. Leaving 900 sailors to me.

Fortunately, not all sailors chose to come to the club, but many did, and as soon as they walked in the door I was swamped doing massages all evening.

The very first sailor of the evening to grace my massage chair loved it so much that he came back several times throughout the night—four times to be exact, and at various stages of intoxication. By his fourth and final massage somewhere around 2 a.m. he fell fast asleep, cheeks stuck to the face pillow. His shipmates had to peel him out of the chair. As they escorted him out, he declared his undying love for me in a loud, incoherent voice all the way out the door. Ahh, the perks of the trade!

As the night went on, things became louder. People became more inebriated, my tips got bigger, and the requests got stranger. One tipsy young sailor said, "I want a massage but I don't want to stop drinking my beer, so I will only have one if you let me drink my Bud through a straw through that face-hole thing." Now this may sound funny, but it was highly unethical, most improper and potentially dangerous.

"Sure, hop on!" I said. Who was I to deprive this poor sailor of his fun?

By the end of the night, my hands felt numb and I ached for a rub-down myself. I had worked from 6.30 p.m. until past 3 a.m. with barely a potty break, trading in the need for urination for a $600 payday. Special events were always fun and made a nice change from my regular routine.

Not that I wasn't enjoying my regular routine too. But for the past few weeks I was beginning to think there was something rather odd about a large number of new clients booking massages with me at the gym: they were all very hairy. Usually this isn't a concern for me, but it wasn't normal for military men to be so hairy or bearded.

These new guys had long unkempt hair, with full beards and moustaches and they all had dark tans. I assumed they must all be civilians, some sort of government employees, maybe; but they had to be connected to the military somehow if they were on base. My curiosity got the better of me as usual and I couldn't help but broach the subject with my new client, who could easily have been the fourth member of ZZ Top.

"I don't mean to be rude, but you and your friends are, umm… much hairier than my usual military clients."

He laughed and without being too specific told me they were on a special assignment and were in Rota to train for a deployment. Now I realized who they were: these guys were Navy SEALs, the most elusive species of the U.S. Navy. I had never met a revered Navy SEAL before, let alone massaged one, and now I had a whole team of them hopping on and off my table during the preparation for their maneuvers. They were getting ready to deploy somewhere hot and sandy and probably not of the tropical beach variety either—more like to the Middle East.

They were also undoubtedly going to be immersing themselves into society unnoticed or be living in caves in the mountains, which explained the beards. They couldn't tell me what they were doing and, as a military wife, I knew better than to ask. What they did say was that they had to blend in and that they were going away for a year and would be leaving in the next few days.

These guys were the nameless, faceless heroes we hear about on CNN—covert and mysterious; I didn't even know my clients' real names. But, I did know I was in awe of them. As I massaged them for the last time before their deployment I thought about how they would soon be in harm's way, separated from family and civilization. I couldn't help thinking that I could be the last human touch they would feel for a very long time. Maybe ever. That was a sobering thought and I was choked up and scared for them. I am sure they could see I was sad; I wasn't very good at hiding my feelings.

As masseuse to the troops, that wasn't the only occasion where I choked up with emotion.

Once I was massaging a young marine in his early twenties. He lay face down, almost asleep. As I massaged his muscular, tattooed arms I noticed a bracelet—a chunky silver chain—with the initials KIA engraved on it. I wondered if Kia was his girlfriend's name and then it suddenly hit me: K.I.A. meant killed in action.

It was upsetting to realize that the engraved name was

undoubtedly a fallen comrade. It also deeply saddened me when I saw tattoos on chests of names and dates honoring fellow soldiers who had lost their lives on the battle field. What some of these guys must have been through in their military careers was hard to even fathom. I was honored to bring them some much-needed therapy.

Not only did I massage the troops in Spain, but I massaged their spouses too. And their offspring, many of whom were still in the womb. Yes, I was massaging a future generation of mini-troops doing pregnancy massages. And massaging the moms-to-be kept me busy because it seemed like everyone was expecting.

Doing a pre-natal massage is very different from a regular massage and needs special certification. Many salons and spas shy away, saying it's dangerous to massage until after the second trimester, but that's not true: a pregnant woman can be massaged from the day of conception (but not during, for obvious reasons) to the day of delivery (during is OK). So, it was safe, but I had to take the necessary precautions and be aware of the change in hormones, body temperature, and expanding hips and belly which compromise breathing and movement.

I positioned my pregnant clients differently too, because they obviously couldn't lie face-down on their bellies and squash the child. So, to avoid any squashing of children, I had two options: perform the massage side-lying with pillows in between the legs and under the head, or use a professional pregnancy pillow. I always used a specialized pillow because it had strategically-placed indents and moms could lie face-down with baby and boobs fully supported.

I had some moms almost in tears at being able to lie on their tummies after not being able to for so long. I performed the whole massage in that position so my clients could relax and sleep for the entire hour. The look on their faces afterwards was one of pure bliss and utter appreciation for that hour of peace.

On occasion, if I felt that my client was open to it, I massaged the belly, too. This way, the fetus wobbling around inside could feel the benefits. It was fun for the moms to feel little Jimmy dancing for joy. It was fun for me too, and not unlike massaging an eighteen-inch yoga ball—although I never shared that analogy.

It was then that I understood that everything happens for a reason and we were meant to move to Spain. I hadn't known it, but those sailors, marines, airmen and soldiers needed me, as there had been no massage therapist on the base for over a year. I was doing something good—something patriotic, even—massaging military men and women who risked their lives for our freedom. I embraced my new role as masseuse to the troops. My work had purpose again and I was content. I hoped and prayed it would last.

There was, however, also a down-side. Because of the two to three-year transitory nature of the posting of a service member, my clientele in Spain lived in a state of perpetual change. I loved taking on new clients, but constantly having to market and prospect for new bodies was a full-time job in itself. Plus, being active duty, my husband would be getting orders to transfer at some point, too.

Being an Air Force wife meant living the life of a nomad and having to rebuild my massage business every time we got stationed at a new base. Moving around definitely wasn't my favorite part of military life, but I had become used to it. Just the same, that didn't mean I didn't dread the day when my husband would come home and say, "Honey, start packing! We are moving!"

It was only a matter of time…

CHAPTER 17

Rubbing rock stars

"A massage is just like a movie, really relaxing and a total escape, except that in a massage you are the star. And you don't miss anything by falling asleep."

—Elizabeth Jane Howard, Author

WE STAYED IN Spain for four glorious years, and it seemed that my massage career morphed into something more exciting and fun with each passing month. Shortly after my arrival, I got to experience another great perk of my chosen industry: massaging celebrities.

I had massaged a few celebs in my career during my stint working at the casino in Atlantic City in 2007. But I didn't really know who they were apart from the fact that one was a basketball star who played in the NBA, one was a baseball player who batted for the Phillies, and one managed the Philadelphia Eagles football team. This may have been a big deal to sports fans, but I didn't follow sports, and I probably couldn't pick the bodies I massaged out of a line-up. I could, on the other hand, definitely pick out the next two celebs I got lucky enough to massage. They weren't sports personalities; they were rock stars!

Both of them were American, each on tour to support the troops in Spain.

Most bases book a celebrity for the main holidays like July 4th, Thanksgiving, or Christmas. On this particular July 4th, it was a contestant from American Idol whose songs I loved—I couldn't wait for the open-air concert. I thought to myself, *He looks like a lovely, down-to-earth guy; I'd love to meet him. Actually, I'd love to massage him. So, how can I make that happen?*

As it turned out, it wasn't that hard because the tour manager got my number from the hotel across the street from my house. The receptionists there knew me and recommended me to guests who wanted in-room massages. By the day of the concert I had already massaged the tour manager twice, plus two of the band members and those connections landed me an invitation to the Green Room before the show to meet the man himself.

That morning I threw on my best dress and zipped over to the rock star's hotel in my beat-up, second-hand Fiat hatchback, slipping a handwritten invitation for a complementary massage under his hotel room door. What genius marketing! So, when I was introduced to him that evening, the American Idol already knew who I was. "Ahh, *you're* the girl who has been massaging my band?" he remarked.

"Guilty as charged," I nodded. "Now it's your turn."

"I'd love to get a massage after the show but I've volunteered to go in the dunk tank and be pelted with wet sponges by the kids. Then I have to eat and probably won't be finished until after midnight."

"Midnight is fine by me. This is Spain—the locals are still out to dinner at that time. Really, I don't care what time it is, I live a minute away from your hotel so call me when you're done. Your manager has my number."

With that, we took some photos together and I went back to

join my friends in the front row, armed with a round of fruity cocktails. The concert was held in a small field on the base and hundreds of military families gathered on the grass in lawn chairs while their kids were running around high on cotton candy. The smell of Independence Day was in the air: sizzling hamburgers, fried onions, hot dogs and spilled beer.

The American Idol contestant was amazing on stage, sporting his rocker look with tight black jeans and spiked hair, and rocked out in a packed crowd full of soldiers and sailors who sang along to his popular hits. He sang until the sun set, just before the fireworks began. The night went much like this: he sang, my girlfriends and I jumped up and down and screamed like high school girls, we refilled our cocktails and jumped even higher and screamed until we had no voices left. My inner teenager was having a ball and when he came back for the encore, the crowd went wild. The Independence Day celebrations were in full swing. The atmosphere was electric, the firework display was larger-than-life, and everyone was in summer party mode.

Sometime after midnight I made my way home and as soon as I walked into my house I passed out on the couch. What did the bartender put in those cocktails? They must have been stronger than I thought as I felt quite tipsy, and I'd only had three. Or it could quite possibly have been five. Anyway, I thought there was no way an actual celebrity would call me for a massage, so it really wasn't a problem.

Until he did, and it was!

"Are you still up for doing a massage? Or is it too late?"

"Yes, yes, of course," I managed with enthusiasm. "I can be ready in 15 minutes."

Aghh, maybe 15 minutes was a tad overzealous.

Oh God, I shouldn't be massaging tipsy. No, it's ok, he is a rock star…right, I need coffee.

I downed two cups, washed my face in cold water, put some more lipstick on, and packed mints in my bag so it wasn't too obvious that I had over imbibed. Minutes later, with my massage table over my shoulder and a big smile on my face, I found myself knocking on the door of his hotel room. I hoped my smile wasn't giving away my ever-so-slight inebriation.

The man on stage some hours before answered the door in surfer shorts and wet flat hair, a contrast to his Hallmark spikey, gelled do. This departure from his rock star getup on stage humanized him. I was right; he *was* lovely—so personable and down to earth.

He was rubbing his eyes and yawning, so I set up the table quickly and invited him to lay down under the blanket. I put two heavy heat packs on his back—a trick to make the client pass out immediately—and soon, he fell asleep.

Even though I do say so myself, the massage went smoothly —that is if you overlooked my dropping the massage oil on the floor, but I am sure no one noticed. We didn't speak a word, the American Idol and I, for the duration of the massage, but afterwards he said that he loved it, felt amazing, and would surely sleep like a baby.

We chatted for a little while about the bit of sightseeing he had managed to squeeze in during his down-time and how he loved the Rock of Gibraltar—that small patch of real estate of southern Spain that belongs to England. It was so nice to talk–what a charming man! He gave me a big hug, a big tip, and I thanked him for the spectacular concert. It had been a fantastic 4th of July.

I didn't tell him that he was the first rock star I had ever massaged. I wonder if he would have wanted to know?

Soon after I had earned my title as *Massage Therapist to the Stars*—OK, so it was self-proclaimed, but it was true—I massaged my second rock star. It was ironic: no rock stars for the first seventeen years of my career and then two come along in the same year! Really? It's just like waiting for a bus in the cold; you wait an hour and then three turn up at the same time.

I had known for a long time that a big-name band was coming

to town and I was excited. My friends and clients asked me jok-ingly if I was going to massage them and without batting an eye-lid, I said, "Abso-bloody-lutely!" But in truth, I had no plan of action whatsoever; it was just lip-service and wishful thinking.

I knew which hotel the band was going to be staying in—the same place as the Idol had stayed. I also knew the guy who was working in protocol for VIPs on the base and who would be escorting the band everywhere; he was taking them to do a radio interview, taking them golfing during the day and out to dinner in the evenings. He happened to be a student in my master's degree class, too. Yes, I had a hook-up; I was sure he would recommend me for a massage.

I was wrong!

My hook-up was quite tight with his celebrity, saying it would be wrong and unethical to endorse one particular therapist. Absolutely not, sorry.

Oh, game on, my friend. Just watch me. I will just have to make it happen all by myself. But I WILL meet the band, I WILL massage them and I will NOT help you with your presentations in class when they suck!

I am not very good at taking no for an answer.

If he wasn't going to help me I'd just have to use the same strategy I had used to meet Olivia Newton-John two years earlier: Law of Attraction. Focus, visualize, and believe without a shadow of a doubt that it can happen. And so, in my mind's eye, I saw myself massaging the whole band. I even wrote their names in my appointment book for the Sunday coming up.

Fake it 'til you make it, I say.

Booking it was the first step. The second was walking the pup over to the Espadana Hotel, to maybe hang around and have a coffee on the terrace by the pool. The hotel was one of the few that allowed pets and I would often sit in the sunshine and have cof-fee with Cheyenne at my feet. Today felt like a coffee-by-the-pool kind of day.

The Massage Gods must have been on my side because as soon as Cheyenne and I rolled into the lobby, I noticed my classmate with a crowd of people sitting on the comfy couches in the lobby. The lead singer wasn't there but I could tell the others were members of his band—they just had that look. My classmate appeared to be briefing them about the day's events and I interrupted cheerfully, "Well hi there, Study Buddy. How are you?" I knew he would be annoyed that I had wormed my way in, but I continued with, "Hi everyone. I'm Mandy, Ken's friend," touching his shoulder. "I am the massage therapist here at the hotel—just in case you need a massage before the show."

Well, that's all I needed to say because a few of them jumped up and said they were in desperate need of a massage after the long flight and could they book this afternoon? Right there and then I booked three appointments. It had been a very productive dog walk.

That afternoon I massaged the drummer in his room. I think he liked the way I fixed him up, stretched him out and took his lower back pain away, because he kindly invited me to come and say hi backstage the following day right before the show.

"Thank you, I certainly will. Oh, and can you tell your front man that I know he is busy but I can even massage him after the show. I do it all the time when celebs are in town."

Technically true.

The next day I went early to the concert with my friends, Melinda and Tim. Tim was the Executive Officer of the base and second in command. He had an all-access pass so no one questioned his wife and I tagging along.

My bad back client from the day before saw me and beckoned me to enter the Green Room, where the band was having refreshments. He gave me a hug, happy to report that he felt much better after his massage. We chatted for a while and then a group of people was ushered to get in line for the "meet and greet" with the whole band. They were the winners of some radio competition. I found myself filing in right along with them.

Base photographers, loaded with professional cameras and hot lights, snapped pictures of the fans with the headliners. Each person had probably less than a minute. When it was my turn I dived in and gave the lead singer a big hug—no time for dispensing with the preliminaries. In the interest of time I blurted out, "Hi, I'm Mandy the massage therapist who massaged your entourage yesterday. I was hoping you had time for one too. There really is no better way to end the show than to de-stress with a therapeutic massage, wouldn't you agree?" He shook his handsome bald head and laughed. "I've heard great things about you. Yeah, I'd love a massage, but I don't get much down time."

"Well, do you want one after the show? It doesn't matter what time because I live right across the street from your hotel." I handed him my card, told him to call me later, and we had photos taken. Productive.

Shortly afterwards, the show started and there he was rocking on stage in an aircraft hangar on a navy base in Spain: a superstar and his band who had traveled half-way across the world to play to two thousand troops and their families. The crowd was screaming and applauding, so grateful for the entertainment and the support.

The band members were so humble, so patriotic and very pro-military and I could tell they all genuinely supported and loved our troops. From an Air Force wife's perspective, that spoke volumes. They played a mixture of old songs, new songs, rock and roll and country, and they brought down the house.

On stage, my newest clients waved to me from behind the keyboard and the drums, and some of the girls next to me in the crowd asked why they seemed to be waving in my direction, so I said, "Oh, because I just massaged them earlier. I am going to massage the lead singer later, too."

Visualize, act as if, fake it 'til you make it!

To finish off the evening, the rock star in his faded jeans and cowboy boots addressed the troops saying he had heard we had a bar on base called *La Plaza* and he invited everyone in the crowd to come and have a drink with the band afterwards. That was almost two thousand people! How were we all going to pile in? La Plaza was where I had massaged the drunken sailors a few months prior and it was quite a large venue, but it might burst at the seams if the whole audience showed up.

I shimmied out to the hallway and pulled out my cell to text Freddie, one of my favorite clients who was somewhere in the crowd. I knew he was a big fan, so I told him he absolutely *had* to be there. My friends and I made our way over to the bar and got ourselves a beer. To our surprise we saw there weren't a thousand fans there. It was Sunday night and these military men and women had to report to work early in the morning. Only a hundred or so concert-goers actually took the band up on their offer of a cold one at the bar.

Most people seemed too shy to approach the celebrities, probably intimidated by their fame, so when the crowd died down I went up to the denim-clad star as if he was my best mate, put my arm around him and said, "There you are! Did you decide if you were going to take me up on that massage?"

He smiled at me. "For sure. I'm drinking my last beer."

I said, "Well in that case I will make this my last beer too."

Then I told him I wanted to introduce two of my favorite massage clients to him and said, "Wait there! Don't move a muscle, I will be right back." Ten seconds later I dragged Freddie and Timo to meet him.

At the sight of their idol, those buff and rugged sailors transformed into giggly teenage girls, nervous and totally in awe of him. I took photos of them shooting the breeze with him and cracking jokes. Everyone was having a great time talking to a world-class celeb who was really just a regular guy enjoying a beer and a laugh with the troops. How cool was that?

Soon after, as he was getting ready to leave he came up to me and said, "I'm in Room 102. See you when you get there." Minutes earlier it was all fun and games and I was cool and collected. But then, it was really happening and I suddenly felt light headed.

I need another beer to calm my nerves…no, better not. I am not going to make a habit of massaging rock stars drunk…

I raced home and downed a cup of English tea instead.

It was after midnight when I arrived at the hotel looking very professional with my table, sheets, blanket and pre-heated lavender bean bags from the microwave to warm his neck and back. As I set up the table and put my pan flute spa music on, I told my new client to hop on the table and lie face down to start. I then disappeared into the bathroom to wash my hands and give him some privacy. Unlike earlier on, there was no silliness or banter. We transformed from rock star and fan, to client and massage therapist.

Throughout the massage, my client remained totally quiet and deeply relaxed. I, on the other hand, was a tad dazed at the reality of the situation: there was a superstar on my table! I'd like to say that I am not star-struck but massaging someone whose CDs were on my shelves in my home was overwhelming, and I was overcome with emotion.

Thank God he had his eyes closed and couldn't see my eyes well up with happy tears. I had to pull myself together and not drip my tears on his back—happy or otherwise—and for the remainder of the session I kept myself composed and professional.

As it turned out, I wasn't that professional because I had gone slightly over the hour. When I say slightly over, I mean by about an hour. I know, I know, that was bad and maybe selfish on my part—maybe even a trifle unethical—but I didn't *want* to stop. I was in awe of this man's talent, his creativity and his success and if I stayed a little longer in his presence, maybe it would rub off on me?

"Umm, I am sorry but I seem to have gone over time. Just a little bit…well, by a lot. A whole hour actually, but I don't want to end the massage."

He said, "Well then don't."

So, I didn't.

It is very important to listen to one's client and I may not have heard him very well earlier when he booked a session for one hour only, but I was listening to him now, and he distinctly told me not to stop. With that, I indulged my client and took my time massaging his neck and face and still not wanting this time to end, I decided it might be nice to massage his head. People don't know this, but bald heads are actually quite nice to massage.

I know because my husband has one. At night, I sometimes gave him a head and shoulder massage in bed to help him fall asleep. It is really quite lovely and therapeutic to have your scalp and temples massaged, not to mention the occipital area at the back of the head where lots of neck muscles attach. And the ears, you can't forget the ears. So, I massaged my rock star's ears, too! What the heck? I thought, *in for a penny, in for a pound.*

There are actually hundreds of pressure points on the ears which are reflections of the body—it's kind of an ear reflexology. The technical name is *auriculotherapy* and not only is it ridiculously relaxing, it is great for relieving stress. I don't normally give my clients ear massages but then again, I don't normally try to make a one-hour massage last two and a half.

Alas, my second rock star massage came to an end. Begrudgingly I sighed, "I am going to reluctantly stop rubbing your ears now, even though I still don't want to finish this massage. But you have a flight to catch."

He grinned. It was time to go home: me across the street and him back to Texas to his life of sell-out concerts and number one hits. With all my stuff packed up ready to leave, I took both his hands, looked him in the eye and said with great respect and sincerity, "Sir, it was an *absolute* pleasure to meet you and massage you."

"It was an absolute pleasure to meet you, too. And by the way, I feel like a million dollars."

"Good, because I forgot to tell you; that is what I charge!"

I left my rock star laughing out loud and I drove home thinking, what a great day at the office!

In the last eighteen years in my life as a massage therapist, I thought I had experienced all that there was to experience in the field. But massaging rock stars was something new and I could definitely get used to it. Yes, it was a high in my career, but perhaps even greater than that, it was also proof positive that we can manifest anything we want to. I saw that night in my mind and believed it was possible. I set the intention, acted as if, by writing the appointment in my diary, and made it happen. And in doing so, it reaffirmed my belief that if you just "put it out there," it will somehow manifest.

And in the spirit of putting things out there, I will put this out there too: that I will massage my celebrity clients again someday, and that I will also win a disgustingly obscene amount of money on the lottery. It doesn't necessarily have to be in that order.

CHAPTER 18

Daddy's feet

"I should like to lie at your feet and die in your arms."

—Voltaire

s I sat on the beach in front of my Spanish villa in Rota, I contemplated just how lucky I was and how my massage career was forever changing and reinventing itself, keeping me on my toes. Now I was massaging the military elite and doing midnight massages when celebs came into town—I could think of worse ways to make a living. Business was booming in that small fishing town by the sea in Southern Spain.

Then suddenly, after a late-night phone call from England, everything screeched to a halt.

My stepsister called in a panic.

"It's Janet. Your dad had a nasty fall and hit his head on the radiator. He is now lying in a pool of blood and is refusing to get into the ambulance. We don't know what to do."

Shocked and stunned, I asked, "Is he conscious?"

"Yes, but you know what he is like. He won't listen to reason."

Typical Dad.

"Put him on the phone."

A moment later, I heard his weak voice.

"Hello Manda. The buggers are trying to take me to hospital and I'm not going!"

"Dad, listen to me. You may have concussion. If you get in the ambulance now, I promise I will fly over tomorrow as soon as I can get a flight, but you have to get checked out by a doctor. Just for tonight. And I will come to the hospital and get you tomorrow. OK?"

After a long silence, he conceded.

* * *

Dad was one of the first people I ever massaged in my life, and I only did it because he was moaning about his bad back. I remember how he used to lay on an orange rug in front of the log fire in the living room with an infra-red heat lamp penetrating down to help soothe his muscles, and I would rub oil into his lower back and shoulders. I was only about fifteen at the time, and I didn't know what I was doing, but he said my rubbing and squeezing helped tremendously, so he became my first regular client—except that he never paid me a penny! When I turned eighteen, I moved away from England but whenever I went home to visit, I would always rub his shoulders and make him feel better.

After I became a licensed massage therapist, Dad liked me to practice my various new techniques on him; he was my human Guinea pig. His favorite type of pampering was reflexology and both he and his partner, Jean, raved about my foot massages. They even photocopied and laminated my foot reflexology chart, which was probably an act of copyright infringement, but since they were elderly, I figured it was fine.

The chart was labeled with different colors and was easy to follow, and foot massage became their little pastime. Even when I wasn't home they would take turns following the foot map, rubbing each other's feet while sitting on opposite ends of the couch watching T.V. They were 160 years old between them and I thought it was absolutely darling that I had them hooked on reflexology in their Golden Years.

One Christmas after I had just flown in from Japan and arrived at their house totally exhausted and jet-lagged, I just wanted a cup of tea and to go to bed early after a fifteen-hour flight and three-hour train journey. Alas, I realized that it wasn't meant to be as I heard a knock on the door. Jean said, "Now, I've told our good friend, Joyce, how wonderful your foot massages are and that you wouldn't mind rubbing her feet while you are visiting."

I was so tired I nearly head-bobbed into my cup of PG Tips, but what could I say? I sat Joyce down, got some cream out of the bathroom cabinet, and gave her an hour of reflexology with Dad looking on from his armchair, proud of his reflexologist daughter and consulting his chart.

Joyce oohed and ahhhed and even dozed off a few times. I wished I could doze off! She was so grateful, she gifted me a big box of my favorite Lindt Lindor Swiss chocolates, which was really sweet of her. I don't ever mind getting paid in chocolate.

Even though I was exhausted and running on empty, I went to bed that night feeling like I had done something good for someone nice, and it was endearing to see Dad and Jean so proud of my work. I loved that feeling!

After stuffing my face with more than half of my box of chocolates, I went to bed. Dad came to tuck me in and then tucked his teddy bear named Teddy in beside me. As soon as my head hit the pillow, I slept like a baby the whole night. But I woke up with a Swiss-chocolate hangover and a belly ache.

During my visits to England, even though I was on vacation I knew Dad would put me to work. But I didn't mind. I loved massaging his back or his feet and seeing the look of appreciation on his face, knowing how much he enjoyed it and how much better he felt afterwards. It amused me when he grimaced as I found a sensitive spot on his feet. He'd say, "Ouch, what's that?" And I would inevitably say, "neck" or "lower back," and he would check with his map and say, "That sounds about right" and doze back off again. Unlike myself and so many others, Dad never doubted my career choice. He believed in my work, and my power to heal.

After news of Dad's fall, I flew to London on hardly any sleep and drove three hours north straight up the M1 to the hospital. When I found which ward he was on, I ran up the stairs and rushed to his hospital bed.

I saw an old, weak man lying in bed, frail and scared looking up to the ceiling, with a black eye and cuts from hitting his head. He wore his favorite fleece navy dressing gown and familiar round gold-rimmed eye-glasses. His comfy brown sheepskin slippers sat beside the bed.

The few white hairs he still had on his head hadn't been combed and were sticking up. His white moustache needed trimming and Dad was long-due a shave, which was unlike my father. He was meticulous about being cleanly shaven from his army days. Seeing him in that state, I burst out crying and ran to his side. I held him tight, tears running down my face while he kissed my head. All I could muster was, "Oh Dad…"

In a weak voice, he joked, "You should have seen the other guy!" and we both laughed. In his next breath he said, "Rub my feet, will you Manda."

Doing as I was told, I sat at the end of the hospital bed and gave him his reflexology, surprising the doctors when they came in.

I told them I was his daughter and assured them I was a licensed reflexologist. They let me continue, which was a smart decision on their part because I was in no mood to be told I couldn't do it. I reveled in the fact that I could give my dad the gift of touch, and it confirmed to me that my work was truly a blessing. But it wasn't until he was really sick that I realized just how much of a blessing it was. For him and for me.

* * *

After the fall, Dad had a stroke and it became painfully evident he couldn't live at home anymore. His beloved Jean was age 80 herself and simply didn't have the strength to keep picking him up when he would fall. Not to mention, the stress of seeing his head covered in blood after diving headfirst into radiators was turning her into a nervous wreck. And so, the gut-wrenching decision had to be made to put Dad into a facility where he could get the care he needed.

He fought it all the way but he was out of options. Knowing my dad had lost the will to live was more than I could bear. But I couldn't give up too, so each day I gave him a massage. He would sit in his chair and ask me to rub his back, or he would complain that it was itching so I would give him a wash and scrub and then massage moisturizer into his whole back. Dad was a self-professed awkward bugger and even when he was sick, he was no different. He was indeed an awkward bugger with his massages too, and complained about the way I was rubbing him.

He knew nothing about massage techniques and I was the expert, but he insisted I just rub in circles around his shoulders which is what amateurs do and it is completely superficial. But I wanted him to feel better so I humored him with the weird moves saying, "OK Dad, you know best…"

I massaged his hands and arms as he kept his eyes closed. He had no energy to talk but I knew he was half awake as he kept squeezing my hand as if to thank me. I know my touch comforted him; using the element of touch to communicate when words were no longer possible was the greatest gift of all.

In the silence of the room, I was lost in my thoughts. Right now, there was no greater gift in the world than massage. Nothing else had the power to make my father feel better, more comforted, more nurtured or more loved. And nothing could have made me feel more valuable than being able to massage my dying dad. What a blessing to both of us! I realized it now more than ever that it was the most valuable gift I had ever had. Why had it taken me until now to see that? How could I ever have thought that massaging wasn't enough for me? It was enough. It had always been enough, and I am sure Dad would have agreed with me.

It was an unusually hot, sunny Tuesday in June in England, and I was determined to make this day a happy one. Because it was such a beautiful day outside, I made Dad go out and sit in the sunshine. He tried to argue and although I could see he was tired, I wasn't backing down on this one. He needed to feel the sun on his face one last time. He barely had the strength to walk but together, we slowly made it to the little wooden bench on the patio covered with pots of flowers. One of the nurses brought us milky coffee just the way he liked it and some chocolate biscuits which he ate—he was always a sucker for anything sweet. We held hands as we ate our biscuits and Dad closed his eyes.

I said, "I just wanted you to feel the warmth on your face, Dad; it will do you the world of good," and he nodded. Shortly after, he wanted to go back inside and take a nap, so I followed his wishes and put him to bed. I asked if he would like a reflexology, and he beamed so I took that as a yes. I knew that at this stage this was the nicest thing I could do for him and I felt contented.

I gave him a light foot massage and for once I didn't want to watch the funny faces he pulled as I poked a sensitive point. I just wanted him to feel cared for and loved. He fell asleep and so I left him to nap with Teddy, and I came back later that evening.

I had never seen Dad so weak and frail or so tiny, and I hated to see him depressed. More than anything I wanted him to be happy and positive so I brought my white board with me to do something I had learned from Reverend Margaret at church. I said, "Right, Dad. I know you feel lousy and I wish you felt better and that things were different, but we have to be grateful for what we have and we are not going to focus on bad things today." He agreed with me.

"We are going to do a Top 10 List of your favorite things in life," I continued, as cheerfully as I could. "I am going to put this board in front of you so you always have a reminder of the things that make you happy." Reluctantly, he played along and at the top of his list was "*my two lovely daughters*" and then we wrote "*motorbikes*" because he used to love his gold-colored Suzuki and would spend hours polishing it in the garage when we were little. I loved that gasoline smell and would stand next to the bike, inhaling deeply before Dad realized what I was doing and told me to "bloody well stop that!"

We also wrote down "*ice cream from Henley-in-Arden,*" because we would drive there on Sunday afternoons as a family and have homemade ice cream. Dad loved to look at all the different flavors even though he would inevitably choose vanilla. And sometimes he would even have two scoops with a Cadbury's chocolate Flake wedged in the top. He grew up in an ice cream shop in Coventry during the war, so it was his comfort food and he wasn't afraid to overindulge. He had never been very adventurous with food and would refer to things like pizza or curry as "foreign muck." I understand if it's an onion *bhaji* or a chicken *jalfrezi*, but pizza? It's cheese on toast! Educate as I might, he wouldn't have it and so everything not vanilla was deemed foreign muck.

We completed the gratitude list on the white board with "*amateur radio, teddy bears, ballroom dancing,* and *old Coventry friends.*" Dad was lucky to still have friends from his hometown that he had known for over half a century and they all came to visit him. I said, "See Dad! Look at this wonderful life. You have so many things to be grateful for and look at all your cards and flowers—you are so loved." He smiled. As he looked at the mini white board and studied it, I could tell his spirits were lifted even though it may have only been for a moment.

"Do you want some ice cream?" I asked.

"Ooh yes please. Vanilla."

I went to the kitchen and brought back a small bowl. I fed him and he wolfed each spoonful down like he was starving. Which he was as he hadn't eaten in days. He really enjoyed that ice cream. The seven-year-old boy in him enjoyed that ice cream. Although he was weak, with each mouthful his face lit up as much as a face could light up when its flame was going out. After I finished feeding him I put my head next to his and held him until he fell asleep. I gave him a kiss, made sure Teddy was tucked in next to him, and told him I loved him. He said, "Love you Manda..." and I left.

That was the last time I saw him alive. He died in his sleep a few hours later at 5 a.m. I like to think that he was happy on his last day, feeling the sunshine on his face and getting his favorite type of massage from his daughter. Nothing fancy. Just a plain vanilla foot reflexology delivered with warm, loving hands.

My happy ending...

*V*ANILLA WAS HOW my father liked to live his life, but my life thus far has been anything but vanilla. I do love vanilla, but I have always opted for the sundae special that came with three additional flavors, hot fudge, whipped cream and a cherry or two on top.

I wanted the crème de la crème in my massage practice, too: the plushest padding for my table, the exotic-smelling essential oils from far-away places, the hot stones, the heated blankets. And I wanted to incorporate a wide range of modalities along with a myriad of new techniques picked up from different countries, bringing an international flavor to the massage table. I have always wanted the extras, the fancy stuff—to have the very best and give the very best massage experience. And I loved it all!

There is a saying: if you love what you do, you will never work another day in your life. I guess, then, that I have never truly worked. Most of the time massaging my clients, my family and my friends has been a blessing and a privilege rather than a job or a means to an end, and has filled my heart with joy. I like to think that touch will be my legacy and that these hands did some good in this world.

Clients who receive massages and therapists who give massages will have their own experiences and their own opinions of what massage should be and what it shouldn't be. This memoir is simply my experience—one person's story. In these pages are the musings of my life, my career, my travels and my relationships, dotted with some of my finer moments and some that maybe weren't so fine. But this life has been colorful and these musings are the beautiful threads that make up the tapestry of my unconventional but richly rewarding life.

This leaves one remaining question: am I going to continue doing massage? The short answer is that I can't see myself being happy doing anything else, or finding a job that would give me so much freedom and fulfillment. That said, for now I am in no hurry to make any long-term decisions. My newest adventure awaits. I have boxes to unpack in our new home in New Mexico. But I don't feel like swimming in a sea of boxes today. Instead, I think I will explore this place and go get myself a massage. What kind? A relaxing Swedish or perhaps something a bit deeper? I think, today, I will go for a nice two-hour Thai massage—they have always been my favorite. I can't think of a better way to spend my afternoon.

I recall the tiny toothless masseuse on Chaweng beach, and I hope my new massage therapist will be as good as her—the angel who started it all…